D0769210

POLISH REVOLUTIONARY POPULISM: A STUDY IN AGRARIAN SOCIALIST THOUGHT FROM THE 1830s TO THE 1850s

PETER BROCK is a member of the Department of History at the University of Toronto. He is the author of *The Slovak National Awakening*, and co-editor, with H. Gordon Skilling, of *The Czech Renascence of the Nineteenth Century*.

Polish populism, which advocated agrarian socialism by either revolutionary or reformist means, emerged first among the émigrés who had left Poland after the Russians defeated the nationalist uprising of 1830. In exile they came into contact with the ideas of French 'Utopian' socialists such as Babeuf, Saint-Simon, Fourier, and Cabet, and they attempted to adapt these ideas to the very different conditions prevailing in their east European homeland. Thus this version of populism preceded in time, and probably influenced, the emergence of the ideas of the better-known Russian narodniks.

Polish Revolutionary Populism describes the activities and conflicting ideologies of the various organizations, abroad and in partitioned Poland, which were struggling for national independence and for agrarian and social reform. Like the author's recent work, *The Slovak National Awakening,* this book deals with the emerging national aspirations characteristic of central and eastern Europe at the time and with the variety of political and social theories that made debate so acrimonious.

HX
315.7
A6
B76

PETER BROCK

Polish Revolutionary Populism:
a study in agrarian socialist
thought from the 1830s
to the 1850s

UNIVERSITY OF TORONTO PRESS
Toronto and Buffalo

45810

HIEBERT LIBRARY
Pacific College - M. B. Seminary
Fresno. Calif. 93702

© University of Toronto Press 1977
Toronto and Buffalo
Printed in Canada

Library of Congress Cataloging in Publication Data

Brock, Peter, 1920-
    Polish revolutionary populism.

    Bibliography: p.
    Includes index.
    1. Populism–Poland–History. 2. Socialism in
Poland–History. I. Title.
HX315.7.A6B76   335'.009438   77-2840
ISBN 0-8020-5374-2

This book has been written by a member of the Centre for Russian and East European Studies, University of Toronto. A list of other books sponsored by the Centre appears at the back of the book.

This book has been published during the
Sesquicentennial year of the University of Toronto

Contents

Preface

The first – the Polish – phase in the history of East European populism is virtually unknown in the West, whereas the next period, which saw the emergence of Russian revolutionary populism, is familiar to many readers, largely through the massive work of the Italian historian Franco Venturi, which is accessible in English translation. Although a very thorough study of early Polish agrarian socialism has been published in London by Lidia and Adam Ciołkosz, the fact that it appeared in Polish has prevented it from gaining the attention of non-Polish historians. Since 1945, scholars in the new Poland have shown great interest in the subject too. Yet for understandable reasons they have usually skirted round the fact that it was the Poles, and not the Russians, who were the innovators in this development. And Soviet historians have normally done likewise.

Beginning as far back as 1953 I have published a number of articles devoted to Polish revolutionary populism in the period between the insurrections of 1830 and 1863. In the present book, which has been composed with the non-specialist reader in mind, I have attempted to give a connected account of the whole movement.

Throughout I have used the Russian term for a populist (*narodnik*), which first appears in Russia only towards the end of the 1870s, to designate his Polish predecessor also. I have done so in order to bring out the many similarities in outlook between them. And my use of an anglicized plural in this case is also justified, I think. (At least if it is not, why then sputniks and beatniks?)

Finally, I am grateful to the respective editors for permission to draw on the following articles of mine: 'The contribution of Leon Rzewuski to the socialist movement in 1848,' *Annali* of the Istituto Giangiacomo Feltrinelli (Milan) 3 (1960); 'The Polish "Movement to the People": an early chapter in the history of East European Populism,' *Slavonic and East European Review* (London) 40, no. 94 (Dec. 1961); 'Socialism and nationalism in Poland, 1840-1846,' *Canadian Slavonic Papers* (Toronto) 4 (1960); and to Macmillan & Co. Ltd for such permission in regard to my study 'The socialists of the Polish "Great Emigration," ' in Asa Briggs and John Saville, eds, *Essays in Labour History: In Memory of G.D.H. Cole* (London 1960; new edn, 1967). I would like to thank the Centre for Russian and East European Studies (University of Toronto) for providing funds for typing the manuscript of this book, and Larry MacDonald, my editor, who once again provided valuable asistance at various stages in its production. The book has been published with the assistance of a grant from the Social Science Research Council of Canada, using funds provided by the Canada Council, and a grant from the Publications Fund of University of Toronto Press.

P de B B

POLISH REVOLUTIONARY POPULISM:
A STUDY IN AGRARIAN SOCIALIST THOUGHT
FROM THE 1830s TO THE 1850s

Prologue

In 1861 Alexander Herzen issued his famous call: 'To the people.' It was a summons to his fellow Russian radicals in the intelligentsia to bring the gospel of socialism to the peasant masses of their country. In Russia and the Slav world, according to Herzen and his followers, the peasantry, the people, had preserved their communal institutions intact. These would make the creation of a new social order possible without going through the stage of capitalist industrialism. A loosely federated commonwealth of free peasant communities would be Russia's contribution to a better world. Such ideas, through the writings of Herzen himself and those of Chernishevsky, Lavrov, Mikhailovsky, and others, spread among the younger Russian intellectuals and provided the inspiration for the 'heroic age' of the Russian revolutionary movement. Their creed became known as populism *(narodnichestvo)* from its idealization of the Russian peasantry as the incarnation of the spirit of socialism. It led in the mid-1870s to the well-known 'movement to the people' *(khozhdenie v narod),* when young revolutionaries, no longer content merely to discuss but anxious now for action, went out to spread their ideas among the peasantry. Even though the movement failed in its object, and its supporters turned to violence (which also proved abortive), populist ideas continued in Russia until the suppression of the populist-oriented Socialist Revolutionary Party after the Bolshevik Revolution. Meanwhile, by the end of the century these ideas had spread to the other lands of Eastern Europe, where they soon sloughed off their socialist coating.

Elements of agrarian socialism had been present in the scheme for partial land nationalization in the *Russkaia Pravda* drawn up by Pavel Pestel', who was executed after the unsuccessful Decembrist revolt in

Russia in 1825. By the early 1830s the ideas of the French Utopian socialist 'sects' were beginning to spread in Russia, though still on a very small scale: Herzen and Ogariev, for instance, belonged to a group in Moscow devoted to the study of their writings, and from the mid-1840s Fourier had his disciples in the Petrashevsky circle. But the first attempt to adapt the ideas of West European socialism, which had been devised for application in a society where the industrial revolution had made great strides, to an almost wholly agrarian economy and to transform them into a doctrine of peasant, of agrarian, socialism, came not from the Russians but from a small group of Polish émigrés who had found refuge in the early 1830s on English soil.

That there was some Polish influence on Herzen, the founder of Russian populism, seems pretty certain. He was closely associated during his London exile in the 1850s with the leading Polish agrarian socialists:[1] it is difficult to believe that their ideas and experience did not have some effect on their Russian colleague's thinking.[2] Herzen's agrarian version of the socialist faith dates back earlier of course – probably to 1847 or thereabouts; the ideas of the Russian slavophils and the account by the German Baron von Haxthausen of the repartitional commune *(mir)* in Russia were obvious sources for his beliefs, as were the writings of the French Utopian socialists. The emergence of Russian revolutionary populism was not conditioned by the prior existence of Polish revolutionary populism. Yet the larger dimensions and the wider impact of Russian populism should not lead us to overlook the fact (as historians have done hitherto) that the initial phase in the development of East European populism came several decades earlier. It was among Polish exiles who had settled in Western Europe at the beginning of the 1830s and among Polish conspirators in the homeland, who collaborated with them in the struggle against the partitioning powers, that revolutionary populism was born.

The seed from which the doctrine germinated was provided by the French Utopians; the impulse behind its development derived from the loss of national independence. Thus we may understand why populism, whether revolutionary or reformist, emerged first among Poles and not Russians. Polish nationalism[3] and French Utopian socialism were its parents. Its goal was the establishment of an agrarian socialist society after national liberation had been achieved, the revolutionaries calling for forceful means and the reformists urging peaceful persuasion to bring this about. The child, unlike the sturdier offspring of Russian populism, was stillborn, for in 1863 the struggle to free Poland from alien rule ended in disaster.[4]

1

The birth of revolutionary populism

In the uprising against the Russians which broke out in November 1830 in Warsaw, the capital of the so-called Congress Kingdom established in 1815, the Poles were finally defeated after nearly a year's fighting. To escape the repression which the Russian administration now instituted, many who had taken part in one way or another in the uprising went into exile. The number of émigrés eventually exceeded seven thousand persons. The political régime in the Polish provinces under Austrian and Prussian rule, which had not been involved in the fighting, was less severe than under the Russians. But for over a decade Polish political and intellectual life was now to be centred in the émigré groups which gathered abroad, mainly in France, England, and Belgium. It was as a member of the 'Great Emigration,'[1] the term used by Polish historians to define this phase of their country's history, that Chopin composed much of his music; and during this period the great trio in Polish romantic literature – Mickiewicz, Słowacki, and Krasiński – wrote many of their famous poems abroad. But the émigrés' efforts were naturally directed primarily to political ends. It was politics that absorbed their thoughts and dreams, and even the music and poetry of the giants were suffused with political meaning.

The challenge of emigration proved germinal in the realm of political ideas. The problem of Poland's independence, of course, dominated the whole of the émigrés' political thinking. Though some of the leaders of the conservative camp wished to confine the discussion within a purely political framework, that proved impossible. The question of regaining their country's independence could not be separated from other issues. Why, in the first place, had Poland lost its freedom at the end of the eighteenth century? And why had the recent uprising failed to restore it? A question of political tactics now broadened out into an examination of underlying social and economic factors. The failure of the insurrectionary government to enlist the wholehearted support of the peasantry was seen by many as a prime cause of defeat. To rally the peasant masses behind the nationalist movement throughout the territories formerly comprised within the pre-partition Polish commonwealth (where, except in the Prussian areas, serfdom still prevailed as in the rest of Eastern Europe) could, it was argued, only be achieved through a programme of far-reaching social and economic reforms. Such a programme, when implemented after the future successful insurrection, would sweep away the old social order along with the rule of the partitioning powers.

The debate began almost as soon as the émigrés reached Western Europe. Very soon, at least three distinct and mutually hostile groupings could be distinguished. On the right came the conservatives, led by the distinguished elder statesman Prince Adam Czartoryski, who had headed the insurrectionary government in 1831. Aristocrats by birth and monarchists by inclination, they were never very numerous among the émigrés, but they made up in influence, especially with ruling circles in France and England, what they lacked in numbers. The democratic centre, owing allegiance either to a general of mildly democratic and republican leanings, Józef Dwernicki, or to the historian Joachim Lelewel, one of the outstanding figures among the émigrés, seems to have had the biggest following of any of the émigré groups. But a certain vagueness and colourlessness in its political programme, and even more in its social goals, made it somewhat ineffective as a political force and unproductive of new and original ideas. The émigré left wing was represented by the Polish Democratic Society, a highly centralized organization set up in Paris in 1832, which was to continue in existence until the Great Emigration virtually died away not long before the outbreak of the uprising of January 1863.[2]

The views of the émigré political camps, united only in their desire to win back their country's independence, clashed on a wide variety of topics. Should the efforts of the émigrés be devoted to enlisting the support of western governments for the Polish cause, as Czartoryski and the conservatives advocated? Or should help be sought from an alliance of the peoples of Europe and of the democratic and radical parties? Or, again, should salvation be looked for primarily from the unaided efforts of the Polish nation, as was urged at one time or another by the Polish left? More fundamental than tactical issues like these were the great controversies on the social question, which in Poland's situation meant above all the peasant problem. Serfdom, all agreed, must be ended. But how was this to be done and what was the nature of the agrarian structure which should replace it?

The conservatives, for some time at any rate, wanted to see emancipation brought about by voluntary agreement between peasants and landowners. The latter were to be compensated for all land acquired by the former serfs. The conservatives did not envisage too clearly the political and social régime which might result from a successful uprising; they believed that all efforts should be concentrated on the immediate task of winning independence and that the future should be allowed to look after itself. A liberal constitutional monarchy with full civil rights for all citizens and a lassez-faire economy seems to have been their ideal, derived from the principles enunciated in the famous Constitution of the Third of May, 1791.

In the early years of exile the centre democrats, called by their opponents with some justification 'half-measure men' (*półśrodkowcy*), agreed with the right-wing émigrés in urging a merely voluntary liquidation of serfdom with compensation to the former masters. A final decision on this issue would be taken by a future constituent assembly after the country's liberation. They were liberals in both the economic and political spheres. Wishing to unite under one banner all those who held democratic opinions, from moderate liberals even to the social radicals, they advocated a republican constitution for the reborn Polish state of the future.

The left-wing Polish Democratic Society from the outset stood out uncompromisingly for the compulsory emancipation of the serfs, who were to be given the land they cultivated for themselves, without compensation to their former owners. This policy was to be proclaimed at the commencement of a new uprising and enforced against all opposition from the landowning class, thus transforming a military insurrection into a social revolution. But for fear of completely alienating the sympathies of the gentry at home, on whom the left wing mainly relied for support in conspiratorial work, the landowners were to be allowed – at least for the time being – to keep possession of the manor farms. While in favour of thoroughgoing social reforms and full political democracy, the Society was not socialist in its aims. Moreover, a strong populist note emerged in its propaganda. It regarded the peasantry as 'the vital element of democracy,'[3] which had preserved Polish nationality in a pure form down the centuries and kept it from corruption by Western influences. Its ideal was a society of small peasant proprietors enjoying political liberty as a result of their independent economic status.

A few words should be said at this point about the populistic theories of Lelewel. His historical researches,[4] which he continued to pursue vigorously throughout three decades of exile, led him to the conclusion that in pagan times the Poles, like the other Slavs, had lived under a system of collective landownership organized on the basis of the commune (*gmina*), rather in the manner of the modern Russian *mir* or the South Slav *zadruga*. In the course of time, alongside the peasantry with their communal lands arose a warrior class holding estates as private property. At first, so Lelewel claimed, the two groups were politically on an equal footing. But later the warrior nobility succeeded in destroying the people's liberties and imposing an alien way of life on the nation. The peasant commune then disappeared in Poland, and the peasants gradually sank to the status of serfs deprived of all political rights. The nobility, however, succeeded in taking over many of the features characteristic of the primitive democratic communities and incorporating them in their traditions; it was this that accounted for the creation under the old Polish commonwealth of a gentry democracy. But in fact the people had never abandoned the struggle to regain their rights. The task of Polish democracy, therefore, was to aid them by working for complete political equality and for the restoration of full property rights over the land to those who tilled it, as well as for the abolition of all remaining feudal privileges.

Lelewel himself was opposed to the introduction of common ownership among the peasants; and many Poles, whether of the left or the right, who were influenced in their political thinking by his theories concening the primitive Slav communes (*gminowładztwo*), tended, like the master himself, to regard them as patterns of democratic decentralization rather than as models for a socialist society.[5] But clearly for those Poles who were looking for a native root, an indigenous tradition, for the socialism they had learned in Paris or London, Lelewel's theories provided what they were seeking; and thus it came about that the commune figured so prominently in the schemes of the Polish revolutionary populists. What the *mir* was to be for Herzen and the Russian narodniks, the *gmina* was for the Polish agrarian socialists. It was at the same time a pattern for the future and a battle cry for the present.

The centre of Polish émigré politics in the early 1830s was Paris. In these early years of the July Monarchy, the French capital was the scene of important developments in the history of the French republican and socialist movements. The left opposition included not only moderate republicans of different shades of opinion but also social radicals of various kinds: apolitical socialist sectaries of the 'schools' of Saint-Simon and Fourier as well as Jacobins in the tradition of Babeuf and his communistic Conspiracy of the Equals of 1796, which had advocated a kind of agrarian socialism. A few of the Poles became devotees of one or another of the socialist schools; and Saint-Simonian influence may be seen, for instance, in many of the pronouncements of the Polish Democratic Society, though this body was far from accepting the full gospel. But the gradualism of the Saint-Simonians and of Fourier, their reliance on peaceful means and on propaganda by example and their abhorrence of violent revolution, proved an obstacle to many Polish radicals who looked for the realization of their political and social aspirations to a violent overthrow of the existing order, backed as it was by the bayonets of the partitioning powers. Militant nationalism led all but a handful of the Poles to reject the full teachings of the socialist sects. It is not difficult to see, on the other hand, the appeal of left-wing Jacobin doctrines, in particular those we designate as *babouvisme,* for the more ardent spirits among the Poles. Young émigrés were to be found working beside Frenchmen in such societies as the illegal Société des Amis du Peuple and the Société des Droits de l'Homme et du Citoyen and associating with Buonarroti, the Nestor of *babouvisme* and leader of the left-wing *carbonari.* It is from these beginnings that Polish populist socialism takes its rise.

It is not, however, in France but in England that we find the first organization set up by the Polish exiles with a clearly socialist programme. Until 1834 the number of émigrés in England had been small.[6] About 150 Poles had found a refuge there the previous year after being expelled from Austrian Galicia through Trieste. In 1834 two further groups arrived. First, a shipload of ex-soldiers reached Portsmouth at the beginning of the year, after two years in Prussian captivity following the defeat of the uprising. As will be seen later, these men were to play a key role in our story. In May another influx of newcomers brought the number of Poles in the English capital to about three hundred.

These last arrivals were all convinced democrats, bound together not only by a common political ideology but also by a shared experience. A year earlier, in April 1833, a number of the exiles in France, who were living in the *dépôts* for Polish refugees scattered up and down the country, came together in Switzerland to form a legion to take part in the uprising which had broken out over the German frontier in Frankfurt. The speedy suppression of disturbances in that city by the authorities found the legionaries still in Switzerland. Unwilling to return to France, they remained there as somewhat unwelcome guests and entered into close relations with Mazzini and the Italian nationalist movement, which was active on Swiss soil. Young Poland[7] eventually arose from their midst to take its place in the international brotherhood of Young Europe brought into being through Mazzini's inspiration. The Poles took a leading part in the unsuccessful expedition which the Italian nationalists organized from Swiss territory in February 1834 against the neighbouring king- dom of Piedmont-Sardinia. As a result, the continued presence of the Poles in their country now seemed undesirable to the Swiss authorities, who succeeded in dispatching most of them across France to England. In London, where they now settled, they soon dominated the General Assembly of the Polish Emigration (Ogół Emigracji Polskiej) which the exiles had set up in the capital shortly before.

Most of these newcomers at first supported General Dwernicki's Na- tional Committee of the Polish Emigration, with its headquarters in Paris. 'The Democratic Society [writes one of them] had no attraction for us, since we were afraid that sooner or later it would turn itself into an exclusive sect and occupy a separatist position in the emigration.'[8] Apart from a handful of monarchists, however, the overwhelming ma- jority of the members of the General Assembly professed some form of political radicalism. As the 'Declaration of Faith' (Akt wiary) issued by the General Assembly on 1 September states:

We declare ourselves to be republicans of pure democratic principles, who recog- nise only the majesty of the sovereignty (wszechwładztwo) of the nation's will. The nation is sovereign, the government is its creation and its property. The public official is the servant of the nation, the government and the official are re- vocable at any moment ... The sovereignty of the people is unlimited, its will suffices to revoke a mandate. The guarantee of the justice of such accountability rests on the civil wisdom of the masses, for the people are infallible in their judg- ments and in their demands.

There was no room for privilege of any sort except in so far as it flowed directly from 'virtue and service to society.' 'We aim at equality,' not a mere equality before the law which the division of society into unequal social classes makes a pretence, 'but at that democratic social equality which knows no difference between gentleman and proletarian. We aim at national emancipation.' After Poland's independence had been re- stored within the pre-1772 boundaries, the will of the majority must be respected by all; however, this majority must see that the democratic freedoms were preserved – otherwise a tyranny of the executive power would ensue. 'In addition to the most far-reaching tolerance for all religious denominations, we desire toleration of political opinions, for there lies ... the basis for freedom of thought and of the spoken and written word.' Only in the case of clearly anti-social opinions should any restrictions be imposed.

These were the principles, the Declaration concludes, on the basis of which the members of the General Assembly wished to unite their fellow émigrés – apart from those still cleaving to the old aristocratic order of things. 'On such principles we aim to carry out a life-giving revolution in Poland ... In such a spirit we desire to raise our motherland from the grave and restore to her her lofty calling as leader in the social field for the whole of Slavdom.'

By implication, the Declaration condemned serfdom and hinted at endowing the peasantry with the land. But there is a certain lack of clarity here, an ambiguity and halfheartedness which contrasts with the strong stand taken against any restriction of political liberty. This hesitation can be seen in the section on the agrarian problem:

We further protest against all endowments by kings whensoever reigning on Polish soil, against all investitures, gifts in vassalage of entails and similar feudal misappropriations, where the prize has usually fallen to the instrument of oppression. We protest against this lavishness from which the oligarchy of the so-called Commonwealth has profited. No one except the nation has a right to dispose of its most valued and undoubted property: the Polish soil which the nation has made fertile through the sweat of its brow.[9]

An ardent nationalism is the keynote of the document. No clear distinction is made between the two concepts of 'the nation' and 'the people.' Indeed, the idea of the people seems to embrace all classes within the national community, not merely the labouring classes in town and countryside. Written in the spirit of the French radical republican tradition, drawing inspiration, too, from Mazzini's doctrine of the mission possessed by each nation within the general harmony of mankind's progress, the Declaration yet fell short of the revolutionary socialist doctrines which a small section among its own members had come by this time to hold.

It is among this group that we find the men who may well lay claim to the title of founding fathers of Polish agrarian socialism, indeed to being the first conscious populists of Eastern Europe. Stanisław Worcell[10] was perhaps the most outstanding personality among them; a titled aristocrat by birth, a deputy in the insurrectionary diet, he had hitherto been connected with the émigré centre. But his association with leaders of the left-wing *carbonari* before his successive expulsions from France and Belgium may account for his rapid political evolution towards the left after coming to England in April 1834. Arriving in London he had been largely responsible for organizing the Poles he found there into the General Assembly, together with his colleague Kazimierz Aleksander Pułaski, who had shared his experience of a French prison and expulsion by the authorities of two liberal democracies. Pułaski was an ex-Piarist monk, and this frocked revolutionary, a potential Polish Lamennais, is a somewhat enigmatic figure about whom we would like to know more.[11] He had been a vice-president of the radical Patriotic Society during the November insurrection. In exile he appears as a founder-member of the Polish Democratic Society in Paris; his thoroughgoing radicalism, however, soon led to his exclusion from the Society. Mention should be made here of two other members of the extreme left-wing group among the Poles in London, who were to be important later, though at first they seem to have played only a subordinate role: Zeno Świętosławski,[12] scion of a well-to-do gentry family, who was to become the leading theorist of Polish agrarian socialism, and Seweryn Dziewicki.[13] Dziewicki, unlike the others in this group, who had come to England as individuals, belonged to the 'Swiss' contingent, and presumably at first shared their more moderate political opinions, though he moved rapidly to the left after his arrival there.[14] Finally comes Tadeusz Krępowiecki, probably at first the most influential of them in moulding the ideology of agrarian socialism.[15] Krępowiecki, like Father Pułaski, had been prominent in the radical Patriotic Society during the insurrection; in exile he had passed through the Democratic Society and was closely associated with the left-wing *carbonari,* which had earned him expulsion from France; he had finally ended up in London.

Before his arrival in England Krępowiecki had already acquired the reputation of a dangerous agitator and a propagator of subversive ideas. Most notorious of his utterances at this period was the speech he made in French at a public meeting held in Paris on 29 November 1832 on the second anniversary of the outbreak of the recent uprising. In it, and in the footnotes attached to the published version, Krępowiecki was remarkably outspoken, not only castigating the conduct of the war by the Polish civil and military authorities but also condemning root and branch the whole political and social structure of his country. He painted in darkest colours the plight of the Polish peasantry and the class selfishness of the landowning gentry, comparing the lot of the serf peasant in the eastern territories of the former Polish commonwealth to that of the primitive African – much to the disadvantage of the former: 'La destinée d'un animal est préférable à celle d'un serf lithuanien. Courbé sous le knout d'un surveillant qui le frappe par fantaisie, exploité par son tyran domestique, il l'est encore par le tyran en chef, le czar.' The landowning class, both magnates and lesser gentry, was an excrescence on the Polish body politic: 'L'institution de la noblesse est tout-à-fait anti-nationale.' When the uprising broke out in 1830 the only sound policy, claimed Krępowiecki, would have been to declare a clean break with the past, to proclaim as the insurrectionary government's objective a new political and social order as well as national independence. 'La simple raison disait: Proclamez les droits de l'homme et du citoyen; combattez au nom de la liberté et de l'égalité; donnez la propriété aux paysans; faites par-là une guerre nationale.' But official incompetence and class egoism prevented any measures being taken towards this end. The uprising, which in Krępowiecki's view had had a good chance of success, failed. Poland had again disappeared. 'Elle périt par les hommes qui se saisirent du pouvoir, et qui ne surent enfanter aucune grande idée, aucune pensée revolutionnaire.'[16]

In the picture painted by Krępowiecki in his discourse on conditions in pre-Christian Poland we can see the influence of both eighteenth-century 'primitivism' and the prevalent romanticism, and also that of the theories of Lelewel (becoming extremely popular, as we know, among the émigrés) with respect to the peasant commune, which the latter's historical researches led him to detect in Poland in pagan times. In his harsh delineation of class antagonisms in Polish society Krępowiecki shows traces of the *babouvisme* with which he had come into contact in the French revolutionary underground. Landowning gentry and serf peasant, not factory owner and industrial proletarian, were of course the antagonists in Krępowiecki's scheme of thought, as they had also been originally to some extent in Babeuf's mind. We see, too, an idealization in general of the peasant, combined with the call to better his political and social status, which provides a link between the romantic literary cult of the 'folk', going back into the previous century, and the social revolutionary populism which would find its culmination in the Russian populist movement.

Krępowiecki's speech, naturally enough, evoked cries of outraged protest from his fellow Poles. 'Fouling one's own nest' was the reaction of some on the left as well as of the whole centre and right. Krępowiecki was at this time still a member of the recently founded Polish Democratic Society; the democrats, however, were unwilling to allow the speech to appear under their imprint and in the end money for publishing was provided by the Amis du Peuple.[17] There had been indeed an ambiguous phrase in the foundation declaration of the Society, issued on 17 March 1832,[18] which was to give rise to misunderstanding then and later; echoing Rousseau and the *babouvistes*, it had spoken of 'the land and its fruits common to all' (wspólna dla wszystkich ziemia i jej owoce). Almost certainly this was not intended as a declaration in favour of the nationalization of the land. But it was now interpreted as such by young social radicals like Krępowiecki, and after their expulsion from the Society within a year of its foundation the phrase was still to prove over the years a rallying cry for the socialist elements which were to spring up from time to time within the Society's ranks. Nevertheless, for all its political and social radicalism, and even though its ideology was not uninflueunced – as has been noted – by the Saint-Simonians, the Democratic Society in the 1830s and 1840s was to stand squarely in favour of endowing the peasants with private property rights in the land they cultivated.

Krępowiecki, then, was probably most responsible for the programme which the radical opposition group among the London Poles began to put forward in the summer of 1834. Members of this group started to hold private meetings for discussion in a public house in the city, finally forming themselves into a club (which seems to have acted as a screen for a secret *carbonari* group in which Pułaski, Worcell, and Krępowiecki held sway). Elections were due to take place towards the end of August for the General Assembly's Executive Commission, and, owing perhaps to political apathy among the rank-and-file, members of the club won a majority of seats on this body. Their defeat rallied the 'Swiss' contingent, whose political views were clearly much closer than those of the club to the majority of the membership. One of the main issues dividing the two groups of activists had arisen over the statutes of the General Assembly, which were up for revision. The political philosophy behind the statutes was the same as that expressed in the Declaration of Faith; one clause of the statutes, however, was singled out for special attack by the radicals' club. Article 8 stated: 'No one may be persecuted or called to account for any opinions in whatever manner they may be revealed.'[19] The object of this article is obvious: to make it possible to unite within one organization all Polish émigrés of democratic sympathies and even to leave a loophole, perhaps, for ultimately bringing in the right wing.

For the radicals of the club this was treachery to the cause, a sell-out to Czartoryski and the conservatives. They noted that there were several monarchists within the General Assembly, that Czartoryski had a most capable agent in London at this time in the person of Professor Krystyn Lach Szyrma, and that the administration of the recent grant from the British Parliament for the support of the Polish refugees had been placed in the hands of Czartoryski's English friends, organized in the Literary Association of the Friends of Poland, with whom therefore the General Assembly had to reckon.[20] These facts confirmed the suspicions of the club that their opponents were dishonest in asserting that they, too, were democrats out to establish 'the sovereignty of the people' in their native land. The leftists in the General Assembly opposed any spirit of compromise: 'The left [writes Dziewicki] considered that any opinions contrary to democracy were merely those of traitors and could not be tolerated ... In the spirit of the extreme, Polish democracy can follow only one road ... The nation is not simply where there is a majority; nor organization simply where there are people. Nation and organization are where is to be found a great thought, untampered with and unblemished.'[21]

Towards the end of August 1834, after the opponents of the club had succeeded in having the previous elections to the Executive Commission annulled, new ones were held in which the club's candidates were soundly defeated. Thereupon Krępowiecki, Worcell, Pułaski, Dziewicki, Świętosławski, and fifty-nine others (all of them members of the gentry or the intelligentsia) resigned from the General Assembly and formed a new organization to which they gave the name London Commune (*Gmina Londyńska*). Feelings ran high between former colleagues. Challenges to duel passed from side to side; and charges of 'terrorism' and 'counter-revolutionary' activities were exchanged. The schism was complete.[22]

What was the political credo of the new organization? In what way did its views on society differ from those of the majority of the London Poles?

They were democrats, not liberals, they emphasized repeatedly. Their aim was not unrestricted liberty of thought and action for the individual but to exercise control in the interests of the community. 'For victory, not numbers but dedication is needed, that self-sacrifice which is impossible for an individualist. With several hundred dedicated persons ready to die for the idea which welds them together, and ... inspired by one spirit, it is easier to snatch victory than with several thousands' who have no such discipline. Political and social equality can be firmly established only if its enemies are ruthlessly suppressed. 'The principle of equal rights, equality between all the inhabitants of the Polish lands, abolition of the harmful division into gentry, townspeople, peasants, Jews, is also for all of us something already decided and beyond all doubt'. Any attempt, therefore, to dispute such matters – to limit the restoration of an independent Polish state within the boundaries of the Congress Kingdom, for instance, or to leave the solution of the peasant question to the good will of the landowning class, as the conservatives proposed – must be dealt with forcibly. 'Though we are a minority, we possess something more important than numerical preponderance; we have behind us the complete right, loyalty to principles ... to the idea of struggle with our internal enemy, the aristocracy.' Even in more peaceful times – and it must always be borne in mind, they add, that we live under revolutionary conditions (*w stanie rewolucyjnym*) – popular democracy is not based merely on counting heads. 'We consider it a false position to seek the will of any body in its numerical majority, and not in the idea, in the concept of the necessary, in zeal.'

The achievement of complete political equality was only half the task of the revolutionary élite. More important was to establish, in the words of their contemporary, Voyer d'Argenson, 'l'égalité des conditions sociales,' a phrase the early Polish socialists were to quote so frequently. For without social democracy, political equality became merely a façade to hide the economic subjection of the masses to the propertied classes. The London Commune therefore summoned the Polish emigration to give careful consideration to the whole question of property rights; in the meantime, it came out clearly in favour of a socialist solution. The so-called sacred rights of property sanctified by long tradition, it stated, were based on nothing firmer than class egoism. This was the only conclusion to be drawn from an impartial examination of the laws of inheritance:

We take the liberty today to draw your attention to the following two points: (*i*) the necessity of abolishing the law of inheritance, (*ii*) the necessity of making provision for all members of the national society (*towarzystwo narodowe*), men and women, as soon as they come of age. The national society is obliged to give each of its members tools for the work to which he is trained, and to give him in addition the opportunity to work without being dependent on others. A fund for such endowments will be found in the great landed estates. It is not enough to secure to all members equality before the law and in political rights (this even the *Chronicle* [the organ of the Polish conservatives in exile] promises), but in addition one needs to turn this equality into a reality, aiming through institutions towards equality of property for all ... Property is at the centre of all the evil which oppresses mankind at present; our private and political faults almost all take their beginning from property. Property divides men into hostile camps; it rends the unity of the family of mankind; ... it teaches men to judge institutions not by their usefulness for the whole body but from their convenience to individuals.

Finally the Commune returned to the idea, shared by their opponents in the General Assembly and deriving probably from Herder by way of Mickiewicz and Mazzini, of Poland's 'social mission' to Slavdom and to mankind. Every nation, the Commune proclaimed, incorporates some great idea which marks its contribution to the family of nations. This is the chief justification for inscribing national independence on their banner. 'It would be unforgivable nonsense to wish to raise a nation from the grave or to create one anew without some mission for humanity.' But the nature of Poland's mission had changed. Formerly, before the partitions, it was to defend Christendom against Islam. Now it is different. The sufferings of its people have given it the right to lead all Slavdom (which, unlike the nations of Western Europe, had hitherto contributed nothing to contemporary civilization) in bringing about 'the emancipation of the peoples, in uniting mankind into one family through the introduction of brotherhood not now among individuals, but between great masses.' For the spirit of brotherhood had remained alive in Eastern Europe; whereas the West was individualistic, its peoples had not known fraternity. 'The French Revolution at the end of last century was the John the Baptist of the new faith and till now the Christ has not appeared ... This Christ will not be an individual man but some great nation which, having assimilated everything truly good in the achievements of all its predecessors, and having created from this an ordered whole, will bring to humanity a new social faith. Why should not Slavdom be this Christ of the new faith?' The task of Poland, of all Slavdom, was to complete the revolution begun in France in 1789, to perfect the social teachings developed in recent years among the French with such success. Poland was to be the Messiah of the new socialist world order.[23]

A highly centralized and authoritarian revolutionary élite[24] working to achieve an egalitarian political order and a socialist economy: this in brief was the Commune's programme. It belonged in the revolutionary

tradition running from Babeuf through Buonarroti and Blanqui to Tka-
chev and Lenin, which has been described as the tradition of
'totalitarian Messianic democracy.'[25] In the key role it assigns to economic conditions and to class struggle this programme foreshadowed the
theories of the Marxists; in its primary concern for the land it linked up
with the later populist tradition of the Russian narodniks.

At first the Commune, which had acted hitherto on its own, aimed at
establishing contact with the Polish Democratic Society, which had
rebuffed all attempts at union fron the side of the centrists. The Commune seems to have felt an affinity between its own political creed and
that of the Society, mistakenly as it proved since – whatever the views of
a minority of the rank-and-file – the Society's leadership at least had set
its face sternly against any compromise with socialist doctrines. But at
this moment the democrats were going through an ideological crisis. It
was not yet certain with whom authority in the organization would
eventually lie. Men like Krępowiecki and Pułaski, therefore, who had
been so closely connected with the Society's inauguration, may now
have hoped, despite their previous defeat and expulsion, to be able to
gain control over it and to guide its policy towards a socialist goal along
the lines set out in the Commune's programme.

At first the Commune was full of optimism. Dziewicki writes of plans
to establish a lithographed 'political journal, which will be sent into the
Slav countries.'[26] Nothing appears to have come of this scheme. But
now, nearer home, a spendid opportunity seemed to offer of spreading
the gospel among 'the people.' For the story of how the extreme radicals
of the Polish Commune in London, all of them gentry, came to create as
a vehicle for their political and social ideas the organization known as
the 'Polish People' (*Lud Polski*), for the first time advancing among East
Europeans a programme of agrarian, peasant socialism, we must turn
our attention from London to Portsmouth, where a colony of Polish ex-
soldiers had been established since the beginning of the year.[27]

The Portsmouth group consisted of 212 former private soldiers and
non-commissioned officers, most of them of peasant origin with a sprin-
kling of artisans and small craftsmen.[28] They had taken part in the insurrection and on its defeat had crossed the border into Prussian territory with several thousand officers and men. Whereas the officers seem
in many cases to have been well treated, the Prussians succeeded by
harsh measures in forcing most of the rank-and-file back to the Russian-occupied Congress Kingdom. Those who refused to yield to such
pressure were kept in captivity for more than two years, and finally in

the autumn of 1833 packed off on three ships bound for the United States. Storms separated the vessels in the North Sea and caused them eventually to take shelter in French or English ports. From there the men refused to proceed any further, not wishing to be cut off by the ocean from the possibility of taking part in future efforts to help regain their country's independence. In this the three groups were supported by all sections of the emigration. While the soldiers on two of the ships either found refuge in France or joined the French forces fighting in Algeria, those on the *Marianne*, which had docked in Portsmouth, eventually gained permission from the British authorities to settle in that town.[29]

Even before they had disembarked in Portsmouth early in February 1834 the soldier's fate had been of great concern to the political leaders among the Polish exiles. The overwhelming majority of the members of the Great Emigration came from the landowning class; a few of these were wealthy titled aristocrats, but most belonged to the medium and small gentry. Less than one-quarter of the émigrés, it would seem, were of artisan or peasant origin; and these plebeians were scattered throughout Western Europe among the dozens of small groups in which the Poles were settled. Thus despite its small size, a compact and well-disciplined body of over two hundred men, almost all native sons of the soil, had a special significance; a struggle now ensued to win their political allegiance.

The contest at the beginning lay between Czartoryski and the conservatives on one side and General Dwernicki and his moderate democrats on the other. Doubting if they could remain together indefinitely on English soil, Czartoryski had originally urged the soldiers to join up as a group in the French Foreign Legion in Algiers, where a Polish brigade had existed since 1832. The Portsmouth soldiers, backed by General Dwernicki and his centre democrats, whose emissary in the port was a certain Captain Franciszek Stawiarski, stubbornly refused all pressure to accept the Algerian offer. Why, they asked, should they shed the blood of their Algerian brothers, with whom they had no quarrel? When Czartoryski's fears of their being unable to remain proved unfounded, his standing with the peasant soldiers was undermined. Stawiarski, who had won their confidence by assisting them in their strange and puzzling new environment – most of the soldiers were illiterate, and at first none seems to have known English or French – now became their acknowledged spokesman and political mentor. A Polish major who had accompanied the soldiers in their voyage from Danzig, a keen supporter of

Czartoryski's camp, was driven from the *dépôt* after violent disturbances there; and he left Portsmouth for London soon after. 'He fled as if from hell,' wrote Lach Szyrma, Czartoryski's agent in London.[30] Through Stawiarski's efforts a General Assembly was set up among the peasant soldiers on the model of the London one, with which it became affiliated. Two colleagues now arrived in Portsmouth to assist Captain Stawiarski in his mission: a young doctor, Adam Sobolewski, and a radical priest, Father Wincenty Zienkiewicz, a fiery demagogue and mob orator. Under the influence of captain, doctor, and priest, lamented Lach Szyrma, the soldiers, till then models of soldierly discipline and full of respect for their officers and authority, had within a short time all become democrats and begun to 'address each other as citizen.'[31]

It is not hard to see why the radical propaganda of Stawiarski and his colleagues made such headway among these peasant soldiers. According to most accounts their captivity under the Prussians had been a harrowing experience. They had been ill-treated, starved, made to work long and weary hours – and all this alone, separated from their former officers. Deeper down, more fundamental, was the stored up resentment of the serf against his master for all the injustices he had had to suffer from him and his class without possibility of redress. We can see something of this feeling in the manner in which the soldiers (or rather, their political mentors for them) were to address their fellow émigrés a few months later. 'Our General Assembly [they said] is made up almost entirely of men whom the monstrous decrees of society have placed from the very cradle under the domination, the arbitrary rule, and the yoke of the privileged castes, and ... have prevented ... from getting to know their inborn rights.'[32] It now needed only the promptings of the apostles of the Rights of Man to make a Jacobin out of Wojtek the peasant!

But Wojtek was not yet quite a Jacobin. It had been but a mild brand of republicanism that Stawiarski and his colleagues had been injecting into the peasant soldiers, the same creed as was professed by the majority in the London Assembly of Poles. This was shortly to come under attack from the extreme left as it had previously been attacked from the conservative right. After the split among the London Poles, each group wrote to the Portsmouth soldiers giving its own version of events and attempting to enlist their support. 'The news of the schism among the brothers in London,' wrote Stawiarski, 'saddens us since we love you both.'[33] Soon, however, Stawiarski and his two colleagues in Portsmouth came out squarely on the side of the moderate majority.

Meanwhile, in October, most of the members of the radical London

Commune left London to settle on the island of Jersey. The reasons for the exodus are not quite clear. The cost of living was lower there; more important probably was the proximity of the island to the French coast and the ease with which communication could be established with fellow countrymen living in France.[34] They migrated as a group, and within a few weeks most had affiliated with the Polish Democratic Society, the London Commune being transformed into the Jersey section of the Society. Several members of the Commune, however, not wholly in sympathy with these developments, did not join the new section; while Krępowiecki, Pułaski and Świętosławski, who had previously been expelled from the Society, also remained outside, though undoubtedly guiding the section's policy from behind the scenes.

On their way over to Jersey some members of the Commune had made a small detour in order to visit Portsmouth and the Polish *dépôt* there. One of them, Wincenty Wierzbicki, remained on in the soldiers' quarters for some weeks because of illness – and probably in part by design too – being cared for by the men. Wierzbicki was the first 'apostle' of the new radicalism. Early in November 1834, his colleague Seweryn Dziewicki arrived from Jersey to assist in the mission, and when Wierzbicki's health soon forced him to leave the country for a warmer climate, Dziewicki, joined in the new year by a second emissary from the 'Jersey' Poles, Roch Rupniewski, remained on to work among the 'people.' After a few months nearly 150 of the Portsmouth soldiers had been converted to the new faith and formed into a section of the Democratic Society in close touch with the gentry democrats in Jersey.

At first the section proceeded cautiously because its founders feared opposition to open activities from Stawiarski and Father Zienkiewicz, already alarmed by the extremist views of the newcomers and the effects these were having on the men. But their influence with the soldiers rapidly dwindled, and they became the butt of the same kind of accusations that a few months previously they had themselves thrown against their conservative adversaries. In vain Stawiarski asserted his faith in the equality of man and the sovereignty of the people and listed his good services to the peasant soldiers. In vain he accused Dziewicki of shameless demagogy and unscrupulous promises. 'Our harmony and unanimity [he complained to the Poles' leading English friend] have been destroyed by Dziewicki, who has spread dissension and introduced great irritation and fighting among the Poles at this place, both in the barracks and in the beer shops.'[35] The consciousness of centuries-old class wrongs once stirred up among the peasant soldiers proved fertile ground for the seeds of Jacobin communism. By the spring of 1835 a bare fifty men remained loyal to their old mentors and to the moderate republican creed, while almost three times that number were now gathered in the ranks of the extreme democrats.[36]

The source of the ideological transformation which had occurred among the peasant soldiers must be sought in Jersey among the former members of the London Commune. Unfortunately, so far as can be ascertained, none of the group's statements of doctrine from this early period are extant. We know, however, that the Jersey section soon split – indeed, what émigré group did not split sooner or later, and usually more than once? – and that the communistic elements, already in hot water with the Society's leadership, which had recently taken steps to tighten up discipline among the members and in which the anti-socialist trend had been reinforced, were expelled from the organization in April 1835.[37]

In the spring of that year the Society's Portsmouth section finally come out into the open. Henceforth known as the Grudziąż section, from the town (today known as Grudziądz) where the peasant soldiers had carried out their forced labour under the Prussians, it was now so strong that to all intents and purposes it had absorbed the soldiers' General Assembly. 'In the name of the General Assembly [we say] we are the nucleus of the Polish people ... Our opponents will be subject to severe punishment, for it is not the privileged who make up the Fatherland, but it is the people, who labour for idlers and suffer want, that is sovereign.'[38] From the beginning the Portsmouth section made it clear that its sympathies were on the side of the Jersey socialists and showed its readiness to defy the Society's leadership.[39] The latter, however, while regarding the soldiers with considerable suspicion, was reluctant to take strong measures against the only section whose members were almost all of authentic peasant origin.

The peasant soldiers had accepted what they called 'the well-grounded concept of socialism:'[40] private property had no sanction in natural law since the concept derived not from nature but from 'the influence of social institutions.' 'Centuries of robbery, murder and plunder' had made its position in society unassailable. But it could be, and must be, overthrown, for 'like the right to life property is common to all.'

The Central Section [i.e. of the Polish Democratic Society] talks of giving property to the Polish peasant. Who has a right to give property? And whose property is it that is being given? Are not all men children of one earth with the self-same right to life? Individual property is the source of the existing social order and, if we do not have the courage to replace its concepts with the idea of social property (*własność społeczna*), it will forever stand on guard over the people's slavery and act as the wet-nurse of the privileged castes.

But the social revolution cannot take place without violence: 'For, we repeat, 'I came not to bring peace, but a sword.' Only this sword can usher in the happiness and unity of mankind and end its martyrdom.'[41]

The Central section held back at this time from detailed condemnation of the Portsmouth section's views on property, concentrating on defending itself from the attacks against its authority within the Society. 'We refrain ... from comment on the theory of unlimited equality, of community of property. We are convinced that, as a fragment of the doctrine common to all the Utopians beginning with Minos and Plato up to Babeuf and the Saint-Simonian school, it will not find sympathy in the Society.' They would merely remark that these were questions which could not be solved by some simple remedy. By its attacks on property, the Central section concluded, the Portsmouth section was merely handing the Society's enemies on the right the means with which to damage its cause in the home country and to brand its members as anarchists and terrorists in the eyes of public opinion.[42]

By the late summer of 1835 it was becoming increasingly clear that the socialists had made little headway in bringing round the Society as a whole to their viewpoint. Its leaders, in closer touch with opinion at home, were confident that conspiratorial action there was dependent for success on winning the support of the landowning gentry, who would turn against the Society's emissaries at any mention of confiscation of the manor lands. And in addition they believed that the peasantry, hitherto largely indifferent to patriotic appeals, could only be roused for the national cause by an unambiguous promise of property rights in their holdings. For the socialists of the Jersey section, therefore, it seemed that the time had now arrived to break with existing émigré groups and make a fresh start by creating a new political organization standing squarely for a revolutionary socialist programme. Its nucleus lay at hand in the peasant soldiers of Portsmouth. By now more members from the Jersey section – all of them of course gentry by origin – had crossed over to the mainland to join with their colleagues Dziewicki and Rupniewski in their 'movement to the people.'[43]

Not long before this, on 7 August 1835, the members of the disaffiliated section had issued from Jersey a last appeal 'to the whole of the Society.' It is more a confession of faith, perhaps, than an attempt to persuade the recalcitrant majority.[44] They told how in their exile they had thrown in their lot with the oppressed. The pursuit of freedom, equality, fraternity, and justice, in a word 'the happiness of the people,'[45] had led them to join the ranks of the Democratic Society. It had led them, too, to the discovery that these ideals could only be realized through 'a transformation of property.' This the Central Section had branded as Utopia. Nevertheless, only in this way could harmony be restored to human society, for 'the right of private property ... divorcing human thought from the interest of the community, deadens in man all social feelings and makes him indifferent to poverty and the sufferings of his neighbours.' Differences in wealth and rank, as well as political and economic oppression, stemmed from the same source. The answer was simple: 'let all nature's gifts be common to all, that is to say, let common, socialized ownership (*własność wspólna, społeczeńska*) take the place of individual property.' 'All being assured common use' of the fruits of the earth, 'everyone would at the same time be obliged to undertake such work for the common good as is suited to his physical and moral strength.'

The final step in this 'movement to the people' came on 30 October 1835, when the Portsmouth section of the Democratic Society broke decisively with its parent organization, transforming itself into the 'Grudziąż Commune of the Polish People.' The new Commune's opening manifesto 'to the Polish emigration,' signed by 141 of the peasant soldiers, called for the abolition of private property in the means of production and distribution. A week later six of its mentors from the gentry (including Worcell, Krępowiecki, and Dziewicki) – the first narodniks we may say – issued the following declaration of support:

We, the undersigned, who have worked till now for the good of the Polish people, either alone or in common with those who have taken on the name of the friends of this people, accede in all sincerity of heart to the above act, by which the Polish people make their appearance on the political scene in the character of the Grudziąż Commune and take upon their shoulders the initiative in the Polish national cause. By the present declaration we merge with this people, in a social unity, which we consider as the foundation stone of national strength without and a condition for preserving absolute equality within.[46]

The creation of the Grudziąż Commune marked the climax of the efforts of the Polish gentry populists.

2

Polish narodniks in exile

The arrival in Portsmouth of the Polish veterans at the beginning of 1834 had provided a suitable opportunity for propagating socialism. The humiliations of serfdom still rankled in their minds, and their disillusionment with most of their officers, who in captivity had enjoyed comforts and privileges denied the common soldiers, added to their susceptibility to radical slogans. When several of the socialist-minded *émigré* intellectuals, then most strongly represented in the Democratic Society's group on the island of Jersey, had settled among the largely illiterate soldiers they found ready converts. Neither the expulsion of the Jersey socialists from the Democratic Society nor the almost universal condemnation with which their views were greeted by the rest of the Society's membership was effective in deterring the Portsmouth soldiers from following their example. Thus towards the end of 1835 the group known as the 'Polish People' had emerged.[1]

The organization was divided into 'communes.' The Portsmouth commune was named after Grudziąż, the town where the soldiers had been interned: the small Jersey group, all members of the gentry, took their name from Humań, the scene of a Ukrainian peasant *jacquerie* in the eighteenth century, as a symbol of vicarious penitence for the wrongs done to the peasantry by their class. Mainly responsible for shaping the ideology of the Polish People were the four members of the original Jersey group: Stanisław Worcell, Tadeusz Krępowiecki, Seweryn Dziewicki, and Zeno Świętosławski.

The members of the Polish People considered themselves in a special sense the disciples of Buonarroti, 'the first ... publicly to accept his teaching as their own.'[2] The ideas of Buchez were also particularly close to them; they studied his works, especially the history of the French

Revolution he compiled with Roux-Lavergne, subscribed to his paper *L'Éuropéen,* and frequently corresponded with him.[3] The theories of the Saint-Simonians, Fourier, Lamennais, Owen, and Laponneraye, and later those of Cabet and Proudhon, were expounded by the leaders and eagerly discussed among the members, who also knew the writings of such Polish political thinkers in the progressive tradition as the sixteenth-century humanist Andrzej Frycz Modrzewski.[4]

None of the leaders at this period attempted to create a finished system. The Polish People's ideology can only be pieced together from fragmentary references scattered among a number of manifestos, open letters, and other polemical writings. All documents were put out in the name of the organization and had to be presented first to the whole group for discussion. Nevertheless, the leaders' views undoubtedly predominated among the peasant soldiers.

The most bitter attacks were directed, not towards the Polish conservatives, but against the rival Democratic Society, accused of betraying the principle of common ownership of the land, which the Portsmouth socialists claimed to find expressed in the Little Manifesto of 1832 (see p. 14). The Society's advocacy of small peasant proprietorship was in their opinion due to the predominance within it of the gentry and bourgeoisie. Such a policy would lead to the development in Poland of the evils of industrial and commercial capitalism: 'The Society [they went on] wishes to see in Poland instead of the small number of proprietors there today a much larger number. In this way tyranny and exploitation will be multiplied and Poland will be transformed from an agricultural to an industrial country. A caste of monied men will be created ... lords of workshops and stores, avaricious and vile, men without feeling whom Christ flayed in His holy wrath.'

If after emancipation the peasantry were made owners of the land they cultivated, then political democracy (*wszechwładztwo ludu*) would become a farce, a façade. They would continue to elect the gentry as their representatives, since the latter would still have the real power, and this would mean a new form of serfdom. Moreover, why had the Society advocated leaving the landowners with their estates intact? 'The peasant cottager and other wretched inhabitants of Poland, through the preservation for the lords of extensive acres, are condemned without pity to misery or death from hunger.' In time a new class of village rich would arise.[5]

In all their documents the Polish People stressed the social origins of the rank-and-file members and bitterly denounced the oppression of the peasantry in the home country.

Coming all of us from the plough, we best of all can feel the poverty of the coun-
tryman, his needs and his hopes; we would wish, therefore, in the name of our
suffering brethren to tell society the tale of oppression ... Hunger, cold, sickness,
the lash, stunted intellectual growth: these are the afflictions of the Polish people. The possessors create poverty; the propertyless suffer it. In order to establish equality, it is necessary to struggle so that mankind is not divided into two
camps: those who have property, and the landless, a race of demigods and a race
of animal-like beings with human features.

Their country's history was seen as a story of war between classes, the
exploiting gentry and the oppressed peasantry: 'Our fatherland, that of
the Polish people, was always separate from the fatherland of the gentry, and if there was contact between the two, it resembled that between
a murderer and his victim. Throughout the whole world a sea of blood
divides the gentry from the people.'

Justice could only come by force, by a violent revolution which would
overthrow the old order. With the help of a few 'penitent' gentry who
had joined the popular side, the ruling class would be defeated and destroyed. A 'dictatorship of the people' would then take over and exercise
power during the transition period. It would be armed with drastic powers – though no clear picture is given of the nature of the state which
would be created after the revolution. 'Terrorism, the use of the sword to
bring principle into effect, intolerance of all that either now or at any
time harms this principle or can endanger our aims ... There is our faith,
here are our methods.'[6] The Jacobin example obviously influenced the
Polish People's revolutionary strategy. A justification of terrorism was
also found in the Gospels: their conception of Christ the avenger of social wrong is indeed reminiscent of the medieval chiliasts.[7]

There was, they held, no alternative between slavery, veiled or open,
and absolute equality, the principle expressed by Voyer d'Argenson in
the phrase 'l'égalité des conditions sociales.' These words, constantly repeated by the Polish People, could in their view only mean collective
ownership of a country's resources.[8]

In order not to gather in the hands of individuals the means by which they could
make their influence predominate and their will all powerful, the community
will proclaim itself the sole legal owner and distributor of the instruments of labour. The main instrument is the land, which is destined to maintain the life of
every member of the community. The right to life is the only undeniable human
right and in no way can it depend on individuals. Hence the right to life comes
before the right to property.

No able-bodied person should become a burden on the community. Inherited wealth, which arose from privilege and resulted in inequality, was to disappear. The obligation to work at socially useful tasks was incumbent on all; but there was apparently to be no direction of labour. The necessary tools would be supplied by the state through the local communes, since these would be in closest touch with the citizens. The commune would exercise supervision over agricultural production – rather in the manner of the Russian repartitional commune – allotting holdings to its members and reassigning them if any were unable to fulfil their tasks or in the case of death. The conception of the Polish People was very similar to that of Proudhon in the next decade: 'Everyone [they write] will receive for life an equal portion [of land] properly equipped with livestock, buildings, and implements; from such a holding each individual may draw a profit for himself, provided this in no way injures the welfare of the whole community.' In this fashion it was hoped Poland would be shielded 'from the capitalist vultures circling around her.'[9]

Industry, to which in fact little attention was paid by the Polish People, was to be run on a co-operative basis. The credit system was to be nationalized and, following the proposals of Saint-Simon, the state banks were to be in charge of the country's economy. A system of social security was to be set up to care for the aged and the sick. The arts and sciences were to receive public support – provided they were directed towards social ends.[10] Defence was to be entrusted to a citizen militia: 'One and the same moral feeling will infuse people and army.'[11]

Special attention was to be paid to the education of the community's children, who were to be wards of the state and not exclusively the concern of their parents. (This was quite a revolutionary proposal, even in early Victorian England.) The manors of the landowners were to be taken over as schools and homes for children. After passing through the educational system the offspring of former class enemies would be transformed into good citizens of the socialist state; and when this had been accomplished, the danger of counter-revolution would have passed away and the Kingdom of God on earth would be established for ever.[12]

The members of the Polish People constantly reiterated that they were not theoreticians. But their leader, Worcell, did try to set down a reasoned apologia for his organization's thesis that property is theft.[13] In an essay entitled *On Property*,[14] Worcell described property as a social product, its form subject to the laws of change that regulate society and are different from those governing the natural world. Human history is progressive, not cyclic, and has evolved through a number of epochs with

different needs and ends. Whereas in earlier 'pagan' ages private property was an element of progress and civilization, helping to bind society
more closely together, in the present epoch, which should give expression to 'the word of Christ, the gospel of brotherhood,'[15] other forms are
needed. Private ownership must yield to collective property, since equality is impossible with differences in property rights, liberty unattainable
when some citizens are dependent on others for their livelihood, and
brotherhood cannot flourish where society is based on the principle of
egoism. Rejecting, therefore, the eighteenth-century view which defended socialism on the basis of natural rights,[16] Worcell adopted and developed the Saint-Simonian theory of socialism as the final outcome of
human progress.

Despite attempts to gain converts among the émigrés and spread
their doctrines in the homeland, where they optimistically believed 'the
spirit of Christian sociality which the peasant preserves in his heart'
would make their ideas welcome among the peasantry, the Polish People
failed to make much impact on their fellow countrymen.[17] They lacked
the money that the bigger émigré societies had at their disposal for
large-scale propaganda missions to Poland, while the hostility of the
manor house would in fact have made work among the peasantry extremely difficult.[18] Among the émigrés they were naturally the object of
bitter attacks from the conservative and centrist groups. That the ideas
of the Polish People, however, had supporters among the rank-and-file
of the Democratic Society is shown by some of the comments (sent in
from its sections in 1836) on the draft manifesto which had been prepared by the Society's newly elected leadership. While right-wing members of the Society had wanted the authors of the draft to tone down
their criticism of the role played by the nobility in Polish history, in order to leave the door open for collaboration with other émigré groups,
the extreme left urged that the Society should come out squarely in favour of collective ownership of the land, or at least for its equal division
among the whole peasantry. Both points of view represented minority
positions within the Democratic Society; the bulk of the membership
was solidly behind the leaders.[19]

Typical of the left critics were the two anonymous members of the
Reims section who based their case for collectivization on the Democratic Society's own Little Manifesto of 1832 (which had stated that all
forms of privilege were a negation of equality).

What is property if it is not [a form of] privilege; the enrichment of one person while leaving another in poverty; the bestowal of an exclusive right to profit from a portion of the land? This, as its fruits increase, providing more than suffices for the satisfaction of mere physical needs, brings with it the desire for luxury at a time when others deprived of their material livelihood are likewise unable to support a moral life ... [Thus] one section of the people will have been granted the rights which belong to them, while the rest of the people – much greater in numbers – will have been left in the same position as they are in to-day.

The Prussian government in granting the peasantry the ownership of the land they cultivated at the time of emancipation had not bettered the general condition of the country folk, since the dwarf holders and the landless labourers had reaped no benefit from the reform. 'That majority, which had no share in it, remains in great poverty, in terrible distress.' The same phenomenon, they claimed, might be seen in the case of France, where the land reforms of the revolutionary era had transformed those peasants who had come into full possession of the land into 'enemies of humanity and pillars of despotism.' Timidity on the part of those responsible for drawing up the draft must, the Reims members thought, have been the cause of their failure to advocate collective ownership of the land. Such a solution of the social question was the only one compatible with the Christian gospel.[20]

Similar views were voiced by the Democratic Society's London section, which came out as a whole in favour of socialism: 'In theory you condemn inequality; in practice you uphold it ... We are profoundly convinced that this question of property is the question of the century ... that private property must inevitably be transformed into common property.'[21]

Less radical but also differing on essentials from the position taken up by the authors of the draft was the statement emanating from three anonymous members of the Avignon section. Emancipation and the abolition of the remnants of feudal rights were, they were prepared to grant, an enormous step forward. But was it sufficient? What of the great mass of working people, 'the landless labourers, the servant class, the poor townsfolk, the tenant gentleman-farmer (*czynszowa szlachta*)?'[22]

These millions, are they to be deprived of the benefits of the Fatherland and the privileges of that country where they were born, which they have more than once defended, where through want they have [till now] been forced to serve the great ones, who have trampled upon their human dignity and often treated them with the cruellest disdain? Are they political bastards to be cast aside and condemned for eternity to misery and ignorance, outrage and contumely, persecution and everlasting servitude, and to support the indolence and lawlessness of others?

Industrialization, it was true, might help, but it could not provide a solution. In the circumstances, therefore, the proposals embodied in the draft manifesto would only mean a new variety of serfdom for countless persons.

The rich – that is, the landlords – who constitute only a small proportion of the total number of those possessing land, will have in addition to their fortunes in money as much land as the whole peasantry put together ... In time, through the conditions under which the latter are employed, they will bind them to themselves in an iron servitude ... The great ones, having enslaved some, will find ways to expropriate the rest. This will not be at all difficult. It may be achieved either as a result of the preponderance which comes through great inequalities in landed property or by means of various ... frauds, which may easily take place so long as education and culture have not become widespread ... [Thus] equality, freedom, and the sovereignty of the people are nothing if they are not founded on peasant proprietorship (własność gruntowa) and laws to secure it for all time. If we want to abolish trading in human beings let us do away with the buying and selling of the land.

The land should be 'parcelled fairly among all' in exactly equal lots. Jews and foreigners long resident in the country were to be included in the reform. Differences in the equality of land, apart from wastes and mountainous and inaccessible places, were not to be taken into account, in order to speed the process and win support for the insurrectionary movement, which would have to initiate the reform. Some forms of industry, such as mines, would be nationalized. The land, as in the rather similar proposals put forward by Proudhon, was entailed in the family of its 'owner-cultivator' and would pass down from generation to generation as the common property of the whole family. If the family died out, their farm would revert to the community for reallotment.[23]

The influence of the Polish People, which comes out clearly in the comments of the Democratic Society's left-wing dissidents, found a determined opponent in Wiktor Heltman,[24] the leading spirit in drawing up the new manifesto and perhaps the most influential figure in the

Society at this period. Heltman, though a fervent democrat, was strongly opposed to any hint of collectivism in the Society's programme. Common ownership, in his opinion, was nothing but 'universal theft.' Work should indeed be rewarded according to its social utility. But man had a natural right to dispose of the products of his labour as he pleased, to regard them as his private property – provided this was not to the detriment of his fellow-citizens. The community had a right to demand contributions from him in the form of taxes in order to finance schemes of public utility and to support those incapable of working. Though Heltman was prepared to grant that land nationalization might be a feasible solution in the far-distant future, and that rural producers' co-operatives on a voluntary basis were beneficial, he was convinced that the peasant masses could only be won over as a whole for the revolution by granting them the land they cultivated in unrestricted ownership. Therefore the Great Manifesto, as the document became known, despite socialistic phraseology in places – for instance in its demand that the profits of society should be divided 'according to work and capabilities' – and its plea for the democratic freedoms and for unconditional equality and the abolition of all privilege, came down in practice in favour of small peasant proprietorship.

The debate between the Polish Democrats and their socialist rivals died down after a few years. The Polish People, whose theoretical writings were mostly composed within the first two years of the group's existence, drew in upon itself, ceased in practice to try to convert the emigration and the nation to its creed, and became a closed group of visionaries mapping out blueprints of imaginary Utopias. Without ceasing to be socialists, Dziewicki, Krępowiecki, and Worcell, ambitious to exert more influence on their contemporaries, now left the organization.[25] Only the mystic Świętosławski was left to guide the peasant soldiers of Portsmouth from his island home in Jersey.

Among the émigrés, as has been seen, agrarian socialist ideas enjoyed quite a wide circulation, even though only a very small number had actually thrown in their lot with the one organization having an avowedly socialist programme. In the home country, on the other hand, circumstances were much less favourable to the spread of agrarian socialism. The backwardness of the peasant masses and the weakness of the middle class forced the emissaries of the democrats abroad to rely on the support of the gentry, who, however liberal, shied away from any talk of nationalization of the land. The consequences of this dependence are illustrated, for instance, in the story of Szymon Konarski, who was sent into Poland in 1835 to prepare the ground for an uprising and perished on the gallows in Wilno in 1839.[26] In exile Konarski had inclined towards socialism, collaborating with the future Fourierist Jan Czyński in producing a radical journal, *Połnoc (North)*.[27] 'Let us set up,' he wrote there, 'a society based on the principle of love and fraternal equality, so that each with a moderate amount of labour may maintain himself freely and be lacking in nothing essential. Let us diffuse knowledge and education among all – and then delinquency and crime will disappear from the earth.'[28] After his arrival in the home country in 1835, Konarski soon became convinced that the success of his mission depended on basing conspiratorial action on the help of the gentry, which put the propagation of any form of socialism out of the question.

By the 1840s the Utopia-builders and the mystics were dominant among the émigré narodniks. The influence of such writers as Cabet, and even more of the doctrines of Polish Messianism, according to which Poland was the Christ of the nations whose resurrection would usher in a new golden age for mankind, was partly responsible for this development. Most decisive, perhaps, was the disillusionment resulting from a realization that the overwhelming mass of the émigrés remained impervious to socialist propaganda and in the home country only the promise of property rights to the land they tilled would attract the peasantry to the national cause.

The most finished of the Polish Utopias came from the pen of Świętosławski, now the leading figure in the Polish People. His 'Statutes of the Universal Church' were the fruit of several years' labour.[29] The 'Universal Church' was Świętosławski's name for the socialist world federation he hoped to see established; the Statutes were its constitution. With its capital on the isthmus of Suez (an echo of the Saint-Simonians) and Polish as its official language, the Church would eventually embrace all men in a single creed, the religion of socialism and human brotherhood, the unorthodox version of Christianity propounded by Świętosławski and the Polish People. 'Neither the earth, nor its produce, neither the buildings, nor the fruits of your toil, nor the implements of labour, nothing shall you call your property, for everything that you possess or can possess is God's.' The whole economy, therefore, was to be in the hands of the Church, which would establish a central economic planning department. Precise regulations were laid down for the organization of the machinery of government. At least fourteen ministries were to be set up in charge of the various branches of the community's life, and Świętosławski describes their functions in detail. These 'ministries' somewhat resembled the corporations of later syndicalist theory, since every citizen was enrolled in one or other of them, according to his occupation. The officers of the Church, from Christ's Viceroy (*Namiestnik*) at the top down through an elaborate hierarchy of lower officials, were all to be elected by the sovereign people in a complex system of elections and were to be responsible to the people for their administration. Citizenship was confined to the 'faithful'; there was, however, to be complete equality between the sexes. The arts and sciences would be subsidized by the Church. A free health service and research into the prevention of disease were to be instituted. The care of the children was to be a special concern of the Church; mothers with pre-school children would be freed from other duties in order to devote themselves to their education. For older children there was to be a system of universal, free, state education. The type of training given to a child was to be adapted to its capabilities and inclinations. Secondary education would be open to all; and the upper ranks of the bureaucracy would be chosen from the most talented pupils. For infractions of the law only penalties which were not degrading to man's dignity were to be imposed. Corporal punishment would be abolished and the death penalty used only as a last resort for crimes against the state. Prisons were to aim at the reform of the criminal as much as at the protection of the public, and proper health standards were to be maintained in all penal institutions.

The Church, like Cabet's Icaria, was conceived on totalitarian lines. No opposition was to be allowed, no unorthodox opinions voiced. 'Like a guardian angel, it was to watch over all the thoughts and feelings' of its citizens from early childhood. The clergy, who combined the functions of political commissar and party theoretician, were to see that the purity of the Church's doctrine was maintained and public observances of the faith were properly followed. Persons with doubts were to consult the clergy in order to receive instructions, and the latter were to exercise a general supervision over the educational system.

Once installed throughout the world the Church would continue for ever; there would be an end to wars and hatred. But until its role was acknowledged by all nations, until the old competitive order based on private property was completely wiped out, the Church was to consider itself in a state of war, of permanent revolution. Selective service for the citizen army would be obligatory during this period for all able-bodied males, provided they were not opponents of the régime. As each new country was taken over, the poor and the oppressed would be placed under the Church's special protection and the exploiters liquidated as a class. Land and industry would be socialized. Should any nation later revolt, 'the Church will put an end to its existence, will divide its territories among the nations ... expunge its name, suppress its language, scatter its people.'

The Statutes, setting forth a *nouveau Christianisme* filled with a communist content, were completed in 1844, issued in the name of the Polish People, and then virtually forgotten for over a century. Despite the apocalyptic, half-prophetic language in which they were written, the moralistic and religious terminology which cloaks their essentially social content, and their obscurity in many places, the Statutes represent an interesting document in the history of socialist thought.

Polish agrarian socialism had been concentrated in England until the dissolution of the Polish People in March 1846 on news of the outbreak of the revolution in Cracow (which was expected to unite the whole democratic emigration behind its programme). In France, the centre of émigré activities, Poles had taken part in socialist 'sects' from the outset, and a series of minute and ephemeral Utopian groups arose among the exiles there. Most of them made little or no contribution to the development of socialist ideas. But the attempts made by Fourier's disciple Jan Czyński and Cabet's close collaborator, Ludwik Królikowski,[30] to apply the theories of their masters to Polish conditions deserve some attention, especially since in works devoted to the two famous French Utopians their Polish followers receive scant mention.

Królikowski's was an original, if somewhat naïve, mind. His works, written in a prophetic style and crammed with biblical texts, repelled his contemporaries, and make them exceedingly tiresome to read today. At first a Saint-Simonian, in the early 1840s he emerged as an ardent supporter of the communist doctrines of Cabet, whose personal friend and co-worker he became. Cabet entrusted him with the editorship of his paper, *Le Populaire*, when he departed at the end of 1848 to found his Icarian colony in the United States. During his absence Królikowski, as the 'mandataire du citoyen Cabet,'[31] defended the master and his system against attacks from right and left in a series of articles later reprinted in pamphlet form; and he continued in charge of the paper until it ceased publication in the autumn of 1851. In the previous decade Królikowski had gathered around him a handful of fellow exiles to whom he interpreted Cabet's doctrines in the pages of his own journal: at first *Polska Chrystusowa* (*Poland for Christ*) (1842-6) and then *Zbratnienie* (*Brotherhood*) (1847-8). In adapting Cabet's ideas for his countrymen Królikowski added a number of new elements not to be found in the original creed. Indeed, Królikowski's approach to social problems was in many respects more akin to libertarian socialism than to the totalitarian communism of Cabet; and after the latter's return from America a serious disagreement developed between the two men concerning the relationship between communism and individual liberty. Though Królikowski continued to propagate his own more individualistic version of communism till his death, the breach with the Icarians was never repaired.

The source of Królikowski's communism lay in his understanding of the Gospels, though he derived much, of course, from Cabet, as well as from the Saint-Simonians and the other Utopians. Christ, in his view, had set aside the Old Testament law, which justified private property, commerce, and nationalism; calling his followers to a higher way of life, he instituted for them a community of goods. The early Christians therefore had held all things in common; but later the official church, the object of bitter attack from the extremely theologically unorthodox Królikowski, had betrayed its trust by sanctioning private property, the oppression of the state, and class privilege, all of which resulted from Satan's machinations. From them flowed wars and discord. God had given the earth to all men; there was no need for private possessions since man's wants could be supplied by the community. The second coming of Christ, however, was approaching, when the rule of brotherhood and love in social as in personal relationships would be restored. Królikowski's vision was indeed reminiscent of the Waldenses and the other apocalyptic sects of the Middle Ages. The Polish people, he believed, having suffered most from the existing unjust international order, had a special mission to lead humanity towards the brave new world. As a communist, Królikowski was strongly opposed to the Polish democrats' policy of granting the peasants property rights to their land after emancipation. Not only would this be morally wrong, it would also, he believed, be economically unsound and socially retrogressive, inevitably leading to the creation of a class of poverty-stricken and land-hungry labourers.

Królikowski's Utopia[32] was similar in many respects to Świętosławski's Universal Church, though he never described it in such detail and with such precision.[33] For both, man was essentially good. Evil, the product of bad social institutions, of which private property was the most harmful, would disappear as soon as society was run on truly Christian principles. While Świętosławski envisaged a highly centralized state as necessary to achieve this, Królikowski wished to see a devolution of political power. Parliamentary institutions were, in his opinion, a fraud. Central government would virtually be abolished in his new order, and each community would govern itself on the model of the early Christians. All decisions were to be unanimous; there was to be complete freedom of speech; and the only sanction enforcing the will of society would be the compulsion of brotherly love exercised towards the wrongdoer. The most virtuous and devoted persons would be chosen to perform the few administrative tasks still necessary. Class differences and race prejudice would disappear. Women would enjoy full equality with men, and the children of the community would be educated in a spirit of service. Most important of all, property would be held in common and distributed on the basis of need – only private ownership in consumption goods would be allowed. In contrast to the more militant Świętosławski, Królikowski hoped that the transition to communism could be achieved through peaceful propaganda. But he was ready to admit that it might be necessary to use the sword to extirpate the most dangerous oppressors of the people: the landowners and the bourgeoisie.

This conditional justification of revolutionary violence, combined with Królikowski's egalitarian communism, brought forth a reply from his friend Czyński, which was published in *Poland for Christ*.[34] Czyński, who came of an assimilated Jewish family and throughout his life was to be active on behalf of Polish-Jewish conciliation and the social emancipation of the townspeople in Poland, was at this period an ardent Fourierist. During the forties he published a number of books and pamphlets, mainly in French, expounding the Fourierist doctrine.[35] Like his master, Czyński wished to introduce a more just social order by the force of example and by the gradual conversion of the ruling class. The reorganization of property not its abolition, he writes, not equality but variety was needed. In Poland Czyński hoped that model phalansteries (he used the Polish word *gmina*) might be established on the estates of benevolent landowners ready to act as patrons in joining their manor lands to the peasants' holdings for this purpose. The phalansteries so formed would be run on Fourierist principles. Talent and capital, presumably provided by the lord of the manor, would be rewarded, along with labour, presumably given by the peasants.[36]

Neither Królikowski nor Czyński made much impression on their fellow exiles. A much more prominent figure among the *émigrés*, who was also active for a short period during the late forties in the international socialist movement, was the famous romantic poet Adam Mickiewicz. As a recent writer has pointed out, the poet's views on politics were often contradictory, at one period conservative and nationalist, at another socialist and internationalist.[37] He was therefore to be claimed by both left and right in Poland as their own. 'One can understand Mickiewicz the politician only if one keeps in mind his position as a mystic desperately trying to model his political action and thought on his mystical ideas.' His naïvety about practical politics and the fact that he often wrote as the result of temporary emotional impulses account for the frequent contradictions and seeming about turns in his writings.

During the 1830s and most of the 1840s the exiled Mickiewicz was not formally associated with any party. His idealization of Poland's past brought him near to the conservative wing of the emigration, and throughout his life he remained on terms of friendship with its leader, Prince Adam Czartoryski. With most of the radicals on the other hand his relations were bad, with the exception of Lelewel, whose theories concerning the ancient Slav commune he incorporated into the framework of his own political thinking. To the French Utopians, with some of whose works he was acquainted, he was at first hostile. He criticized them for their rationalist and materialist approach to social problems, for their belief in the possibility of peaceful evolution towards a juster social and international order, and for their neglect of patriotism as a primary factor in political life. A romantic, mystical nationalism was basic in Mickiewicz's political thinking. It drove him to become for a time a devotee of the extreme form of Polish Messianism expounded by the half-mad mystic Towiański; and it led him to expect, as did most Polish radicals, that social change in his native land would require the overthrow of the old order by means of a revolutionary war of liberation on behalf of the oppressed peoples.

After the outbreak of revolution in 1848, Mickiewicz's political opinions moved very rapidly towards the left, largely because of the strong support given by the socialist sections of the French working class and their leaders to the idea of a war on behalf of Poland and the other subject nationalities against the autocrats of Europe, coupled with the hostility or indifference towards such plans in conservative circles. 'As he was a man of strong passions rushing headlong in one direction or another,' Wiktor Weintraub writes of the poet, 'he could not stop halfway. He became a passionate advocate of the workers and their cause.'

Mickiewicz's faith in the European left found practical expression in two undertakings for which he was largely responsible. The first was the formation in March 1848 of a Polish legion to fight in Italy beside the republicans against Austria. This venture, however, was supported neither by the Polish democrats nor by the conservatives, and it finally ended in failure. For his legion Mickiewicz issued a 'Set of Principles' *(Skład zasad),* a short document of only fifteen paragraphs consisting of brief phrases or slogans.[38] As regards social problems, in paragraphs 13 and 14 Mickiewicz advocated a vaguely conceived agrarian socialism:

12. To each family the family farm under the protection of the commune. To each commune the communal lands under the protection of the nation.
13. All property to be respected and held inviolate under the guardianship of the national office.[39]

What Mickiewicz meant exactly by these words has been a matter of controversy. Most probably he was thinking of some form of peasant commune along the lines advocated earlier by the Polish People. But it would also not be inconsistent with Mickiewicz's wording to envisage an agrarian structure under which the country would be divided up between the estates of the gentry, the individual holdings of the peasantry – including those who had previously been landless – and property held by the villagers in common.[40]

After the collapse of his Italian legion, Mickiewicz returned to Paris still anxious to do what he could to further the cause of the international revolutionary movement. He was soon convinced that this might best be done through a daily paper that, while published in French, would at the same time be international in its editorial staff and the range of its contributors. On 15 March 1849 the first number of *La Tribune des peuples*[41] appeared with Mickiewicz as chief editor, the necessary funds having been supplied by a liberal-minded Polish aristocrat, Count Ksawery Branicki.[42] Although a number of French left-wingers of various shades of opinion, as well as radicals from Belgium, Germany, Russia, Spain, Italy, and elsewhere, collaborated on the paper, and the Polish issue was not stressed in its policy, the Poles played the leading role in it until forced out by the reaction.[43] Mickiewicz's journal, which harked back to Babeuf's organ, *La Tribune du peuple,* sought to strengthen the international solidarity of the peoples and the national liberation movements throughout Europe. France under the influence of the industrial proletariat would lead in this work of liberation. Though Mickiewicz regarded the most pressing task to be the establishment of national independence and political democracy, he also pleaded for a social revolution, for 'un état social conforme aux besoins nouveaux du peuple.'[44]

In his articles in *La Tribune des peuples* Mickiewicz declared himself a socialist. For the poet socialism had primarily an ethical and spiritual content; it was more an attitude of mind than a rounded political or economic doctrine. Socialism, he wrote, was a factor of unknown potentiality, terrifying to the defenders of the old order who seek, therefore, to destroy it. But, he goes on, 'effacer n'est pas détruire. On n'efface pas les mots qui sont reproduits un million de fois chaque jour dans les feuilles publiques, et qui sont devenus des mots d'ordre de partis politiques. On ne détruit pas un parti politique en l'empêchant de proclamer son mot d'ordre, son principe.'[45] Socialism, he admitted, was still only half formed and not entirely conscious of its aims and methods; but it was no mere negation, as its enemies declared. At its roots lay love of country and the Christian religion – despite the fact that the pope and the Catholic Church had become a bulwark of reaction, thereby losing their moral authority. As a working journalist, however, it was not his business to give a considered judgment on the socialist systems which had been put forward as universal panaceas, but rather to deal with the events of the moment. The main task of socialists was to help the oppressed nations – the socialists of tomorrow – to regain their freedom and not to engage in controversy over purely theoretical issues.

In Mickiewicz's view it was impossible to achieve socialism by peaceful means. It would result, not from class war, but from a war of the peoples. 'Every scheme ... will be purely Utopian so long as it tries to solve a world problem [such as socialism] by peaceful means and to hurt no one ... In order to achieve [a social revolution] war is a necessity, not peace. One must first liberate Italy, help Germany free herself from her past, and support the peoples in destroying Austria ... A free and independent Poland must be established.'[46] Thus national liberation was an essential preliminary to social democracy.

Assorting strangely with Mickiewicz's socialist and republican views, and bringing him at times into serious conflict with his colleagues, was his cult of the Napoleons, which he shared with many of his fellow-countrymen – they had fought beside Napoleon's armies in 1812 – and which eventually led him to make his peace with the Third Empire. For Mickiewicz, however, there was no inconsistency. He distinguished between the Napoleonic idea, which stood for the use of French military might to support the rights of the oppressed nationalities, and Bonapartism, which represented the exploitation for dynastic ends of the Napoleonic legend. What was needed was a fusion of the Napoleonic idea with the social radicalism of the Utopian sectaries, who had mistakenly wished to impose their theories regardless of national differences.[47] Undoubtedly Mickiewicz was also taken in by the future Emperor Napoleon III's use of democratic and even socialistic phraseology before his achievement of power. But his admiration for the emperor survived the persecution of the French radicals and socialists led by Blanc and Ledru-Rollin, to whose party *La Tribune des peuples* had given its support, and outlasted the suppression of the paper itself in the autumn of 1849. Thereafter, while still remaining nominally a socialist, Mickiewicz was to centre his efforts, until his death during the Crimean War, on trying to gain the support of the French government for the Polish cause.[48]

Populist socialism was most strongly represented in Polish left-wing thought in the 1830s and 1840s. After the successive failures of the revolutionary movement in Poland in 1846 and 1848-9 there was little chance of socialism finding adherents in the home country. Though it was still represented among the left-wing émigrés, the Great Emigration was itself only a shadow of its former self. Weak in numbers and increasingly out of touch with the home country, the émigrés no longer played an important role in the political and intellectual life of the nation.

After reaction developed in France, the Polish Democratic Society transferred its headquarters to London.[49] The leading figure in the Society was now Stanisław Worcell, who had helped to found the Polish People in the mid-1830s. Under his influence and that of the talented but little-known publicist Jan Kanty Podolecki[50] – though not without protest from some members – the democrats abandoned their rigid defence of private property and wrote socialism into the programme of their Society. An attempt was even made to prove that the Society had never been opposed to socialism. Worcell and his colleagues now argued that socialism was the natural fulfilment of democracy and republicanism and the realization of the Christian ideal. The winning of national independence was to be accompanied by the bestowal of full property rights on the peasants, but only as a temporary measure, the first step towards a juster social order. Once genuine parliamentary government and civil liberties had been introduced, socialism would come gradually through piecemeal reforms; there would be no need of a violent overthrow of the old order; those who stood to lose through reform would be compensated by the state.

Today [its leaders stated in a passage typical of their public pronouncements at this period] the Society believes ... that socialism must and will bring its influence to bear on the changes taking place in industry, science, government, religion, the family, property relations, and capital. These changes ... however will come about not by coercion or violence, annihilation or confiscations, or by tyranny; but by seeking out and adapting ... the principles and means appropriate for the general need and for universal brotherhood, and by putting justice, education, and truth in the place of oppression, ignorance, and falsehood ... Where the nation is itself both legislature and executive, there the tyranny and despotism of one section [of the nation] over another cannot exist. Let us suppose for a moment that the community, as a result of that unawareness of which some accuse it, errs in enacting or enforcing a law ... with harm to a minority. Will not the wrong done to a part of its members react on all? ... Will it not become a wrong done to the whole community? ... In such a case the people will easily recognize its mistake and, without any violent upheavals, enter upon a more proper course, giving compensation for any loss it may temporarily have caused.[51]

No attempt was made to work out in detail how land and industry were to be managed in a socialist state; but the Society seems to have envisaged private enterprise in industry and the landed estates of the gentry existing, at least for a time, side by side with voluntary associations of the industrial proletariat and the communal working of the land by the peasantry. In an article, unsigned but probably from Podolecki's pen, praise was given to Buchez, an old friend too of Worcell's from the period of his membership of the Polish People, for his proposals to establish co-operative workers' associations, which might also provide a model for the village commune. 'Although associations will not transform the earth ... into an El Dorado ... at any rate they will exercise a great influence towards bettering the lot of the labouring class. To them belongs the future.'[52]

The Democratic Society's socialism therefore differed little from the vaguely socialist radicalism of the school of Ledru-Rollin and his fellow exiles from France, with whom Worcell and the Polish democrats collaborated closely at this time. Its moderate and reformist character did not satisfy some of the extremer spirits among the Polish émigrés. As a result, in 1856 a rival organization under the leadership of Worcell's old colleague Świętosławski was formed, and took the name London Revolutionary Commune of the Polish People.[53] As its name implies, the Commune harked back to the tradition of the Polish People of the 1830s and early 1840s.

The abolition of private property and the establishment of collectivism based upon a revival of the primitive Slav commune,[54] complete political equality, a transition period after the revolution of the dictatorship of the people, the establishment of a Slav federation within a world-wide socialist republic: the London Commune's programme follows in the footsteps of the earlier organization. What was new, however, was a greater emphasis on industry and labour and less stress on the problems of an agrarian economy. This should undoubtedly be attributed to the influence of English industrial conditions, and the British working-class movement on the ideology of the émigré Polish narodniks.

By the beginning of the next decade, and even before the outbreak of a second insurrection against the Russians in 1863, both the Revolutionary Commune and the Democratic Society had virtually ceased to function. With the defeat of the insurgents a new age began for the Poles.

3

Polish narodniks at home

'In Poland,' wrote Marx and Engels in the *Communist Manifesto,* the communists 'support the party that insists on an agrarian revolution as the prime condition for emancipation, that party which fomented the insurrection in Cracow in 1846.'[1] The agrarian revolution advocated by these Polish left-wing nationalists during the years following the failure of the insurrection against the Russians in 1830 was not, however, a communist one.[2] After a successful uprising against the three partitioning powers, they aimed, at least in the provinces ruled by Austria and Russia, at linking the emancipation of the peasantry to the granting of full property rights in the land they had previously cultivated as serfs. According to the revolutionaries' schemes landlords were not to be compensated for losses incurred, but they were to be left in possession of their manor farms. The goal of all the Polish revolutionaries was the recovery of independence within the frontiers of the old Polish commonwealth as these had existed before the partitions and the establishment of full political democracy in the future Polish state. For their plans the support of both the landowning gentry, the most influential class in the country, and the peasantry, who formed the overwhelming majority of the population, was essential. Any hint of socialism was likely to frighten the landowners; yet the Polish left, convinced that the failure of the 1830 uprising had been due primarily to the indifference of the peasantry, believed that only the promise of full ownership of their holdings *(uwłaszczenie)* would rally the peasants to the national cause. Neither land nationalization in any form nor the socialization of agriculture would have resulted from their projected reforms, but rather a broadening of the class of property owners to include the peasant smallholders.

The economic and social conditions of the home country, combined with the oppressive political régime imposed by the partitioning powers, prevented any large-scale propagation of narodnik doctrines in Poland itself. Nonetheless, especially in the early 1840s, agrarian socialist ideas began to find adherents among the revolutionary nationalists there.[3]

The uprising of 1830 had led to the virtual suppression of the autonomy of the Congress Kingdom of 1815. The arrests, deportations, and executions which ensued had affected mainly the upper classes. To some degree the Russian authorities in the hope of winning their allegiance had tended to favour the peasantry, who were economically backward and in many cases barely conscious of their nationality. Indeed, a deep gulf then existed between the manor house and the village. But the peasants had their grievances against the government too. Conscription for the Russian army and the quartering of Russian soldiers in the villages and high taxation and corvées for the upkeep of fortresses and roads were heavy burdens which did not serve to make Russian rule popular in the countryside.

In 1830-1, however, the insurrectionary authorities had failed to ameliorate the conditions of the peasantry; fearing the opposition of the landowners to the smallest measure of reform, they had refrained from emancipating even the serfs on the crown lands. The Polish peasants of the Congress Kingdom had éarlier gained a theoretical freedom of movement by a decree of 1807 when the area formed part of the Duchy of Warsaw. But after the 1830 uprising, as before, the traditional serf economy was still in force, though modified in places by the conversion of labour services (pańszczyzna) into rent. It was becoming increasingly clear that primitive equipment and poor work made the peasants' work unproductive in comparison with hired labour. A rural proletariat amounting to nearly half the village population, which resulted in part from the peasants' increasing insecurity of tenure, provided a pool from which the landlords could obtain a labour force for employment on their home farms. Peasant discontent leading to sporadic outbreaks in the countryside was a feature of the years following the 1830 uprising.

Over the border in the Prussian-occupied province of Poznania, political and economic conditions differed considerably. Emancipation of the peasants had been initiated by the Prussian government as early as 1823, but in such a way as to benefit primarily the well-to-do peasants, whom the authorities hoped would become a bulwark of the existing régime. Many of the smaller peasants were expropriated, and the numerous class of landless agricultural labourers provided a dissatisfied element in the rural population. Owing partly to competition from the more highly industrialized West, discontent was also rife among urban craftsmen, many of them former peasants who had migrated to the towns in search of a living. In the political sphere, however, with the accession in 1840 of the more progressive King Frederick William IV and the desire on the part of the Prussians, especially liberals, to keep the Poles in reserve as possible allies against the Russians in a future war over the unification of Germany, the government began to pursue a milder policy towards the Polish population. Censorship of the press was relaxed, and attempts to carry out a policy of Germanization were temporarily abandoned. Poznań in the early forties, therefore, became a centre of organization for the Polish nationalist movement at a time when the revolutionaries could act only with the greatest circumspection under Russia or Austria.

At this period the most backward of the Polish provinces in almost every respect was Austrian Galicia (in the eastern half of which the population was predominantly Ukrainian). In that region there was scarcely any industrial development; agricultural techniques were extremely primitive; serfdom was in force on almost all estates; and in the countryside a diehard Polish gentry faced a resentful and ignorant peasantry tending to regard the Austrian emperor as its protector against the manor. Only in the tiny Free City of Cracow, nominally independent until 1846 but in fact under the close supervision of the three partitioning powers, did the Polish nationalists obtain a precarious foothold.

The revolutionary nationalists at home were naturally in contact with their compatriots abroad. Indeed, during the 1830s, émigrés had taken the initiative in organizing underground activity in the home country. Young Poland, under Lelewel's leadership, had been the most active, and it had chosen the Congress Kingdom and Galicia as the best terrain for underground work. A series of conspiracies was uncovered by the Russian and Austrian authorities, and many of the conspirators, if they were not lucky enough to escape across the frontiers, were executed or sentenced to long periods of imprisonment. By the end of the decade a change of policy became apparent among Polish nationalists. The more moderate elements, especially in Poznania, while not renouncing independence as their ultimate aim, came more and more to concentrate on building up the nation's economic and social strength. This programme, which came to be known as 'organic work,' could be pursued only within the law. But many Poles still held to the insurrectionary tradition and continued to await the day when another uprising would restore their country's independence. They were in contact with the left-wing Polish Democratic Society, with its headquarters in France, which was extremely influential among the émigrés at this period. The Society sent emissaries to Poland and its papers and pamphlets circulated there. But in the 1840s, in contrast to the previous decade, the revolutionaries at home, while looking to the emigration for intellectual leadership, on the whole maintained their organizational independence.

In this period of renewed underground activity, which was to reach a climax in the events of 1846, a socialist current embracing both revolutionary and reformist populists is clearly discernible. It may be seen in the peasant conspiracy of Father Ściegienny in the Congress Kingdom; in Poznania the Union of Plebeians organized by the bookseller Walenty Stefański and the intellectual circle around the Woykowskis were imbued with agrarian socialist ideas; and finally, in the person of young Edward Dembowski, active as a revolutionary under all three partitioning powers, we have the first socialist theoretician on Polish soil.

II

Father Piotr Ściegienny,[4] the son of a serf, was born in 1801 into a poor peasant family in the district of Kielce. Ściegienny knew from his own childhood the meaning of hunger and misery and had felt the disdain of the rich for the poor man's son. Throughout his life he was to retain the outlook and ways of his peasant ancestors. Despite poverty and oppression, however, the boy succeeded in obtaining an education, and after leaving school became in turn a village schoolmaster, a private tutor, and a clerk in a government office. Finally, in his late twenties, he decided to take orders and spent the next few years within cloister walls. After the 1830 uprising he returned to his native countryside, and from 1833 onwards he was parish priest of a small village, Wilkołaz, on the border between the provinces of Lublin and Kielce.

Little is known of Ściegienny's activities during the next decade. Uneventful as his life seems to have been on the surface during this period, the obscure village priest was growing into the agrarian revolutionary who sought to arouse the peasant masses to fight for independence and a new and juster social order. It is very probable that Ściegienny was influenced in this evolution by his previous contacts with Father Pułaski[5] and other social radicals among the order of Piarist monks, of which Ściegienny had himself been a member for a few years. Undoubtedly the failure of the insurrectionists to win much support from the peasantry in 1830-1 must have made a deep impression on the young priest, as it did on so many of his generation. A son of the village living and working close to the peasantry, Ściegienny was in a position to understand their feelings and needs. Later, during visits to the provincial capital of Lublin, friends introduced him to the radical literature being smuggled by the Polish conspiratorial groups across the border into the Congress Kingdom. In this way Ściegienny read the papers and pamphlets of the émigré Democratic Society; he also almost certainly knew the publications issued by the 'Polish People.' Above all he was influenced by Lamennais, whose works *Paroles d'un croyant* and *Le Livre du peuple* he studied either in the original, for he seems to have known some French, or in their Polish translations. Somewhat naïve in his outlook, at the same time warm-hearted and possessed of considerable native wit, genuinely devoted to his flock and sensitive to the social injustice around him, which was so hard to square with the religion he served, Ściegienny was turned into a conscious revolutionary by his reading.

Early in the 1840s we discover the first traces of an underground organization among the peasants of the area, inspired by the vicar of Wilkołaz, who personally circulated propaganda among the peasants and distributed among them a number of inflammatory tracts. These were composed by the vicar himself, copied by hand, and passed around to be read to the peasants assembled together in the evenings after the day's labour. In this way arose the so-called Letter of Pope Gregory XVI.[6] This document is one of the most remarkable in the history of revolutionary literature; though almost certainly written by Ściegienny himself, it purported to be a pastoral letter of the reigning pope to the Polish people. In reality the pope was a determined opponent of the national aspirations of the Poles, as his encyclical *Cum Primum* of 1832 condemning the uprising had shown. But the peasants believed in the Letter's authenticity. Indeed it was skilfully composed to appeal to their sympathies and written in simple and colourful language; with picturesque yet telling metaphors, full of allusions to their daily life and to their hardships and their grievances, it was a strong call to action to right centuries-old wrongs.

I have cried out to those who oppress you to treat you as human beings and not to crush you with labour services, with rents and various kinds of dues. I have besought your kings and emperors not to burden you with taxes and the quartering of soldiers, not to drive you to the wars like cattle to the slaughter ... but rather to live with you as brothers. But their hearts have become hardened and my pleas for you they have not heeded. Your misery therefore has not been abated, let alone brought to an end.

God created man to enjoy the fruits of the earth and to lead a happy, harmonious, and virtuous life, the Letter continues, but evil persons – landowners and rulers – have robbed the people of free access to the land and thereby brought about hunger, misery, and the exploitation of man by man. Do not believe your masters when they say God means you to bear your misfortunes patiently and without complaining. 'God ... did not create you for poverty and suffering. His will is that ... you should abound in all things, and live together in joy and concord.' None should be ignorant: the book of knowledge should be open to all alike. At the beginning all men were on an equal footing and so things should be now.

The lord is a man like the peasant, owing legs and arms, health and strength to God. He can, and indeed he should, earn his own bread for himself. God, having created man, placed him upon the earth which he had set aside for him and all his kind, allowing him to make use of all the fruits of the earth which he should obtain by his labour. At the same time man paid nothing to God, neither for the land where he dwelt nor for the fruits thereof ... Man was then free as today the bird of the air is free. Later the stronger took from the weaker their land and made it their own ... They dealt out to their poorer fellows small pieces of this land they had unlawfully seized, and ordered them to do labour services and boon work for it, and to pay them dues and rents and taxes.

Therefore, take back now as your own the land which was forcibly wrested from your ancestors. Refuse to render labour services to the lords of the manor; withhold taxes demanded of you by your rulers. Unite with your fellow villagers to regain your rights; unite, too, with the artisans of the towns who, knowing for the most part the art of reading and writing, will be of great service to the cause. In unity lies strength: your numbers will bring you victory. You must, therefore, be ready to regain by force of arms what is rightfully yours. And the army, too, will be with you. 'Soldiers are but peasants or townsfolk; they should therefore side with the peasants and townsfolk.'

Wars of aggression, such as rulers stir up for their own ends, are a crime against God and you should refuse to take part in them, for they bring no profit to the common folk throughout the world. 'War is the worst evil in the world. War destroys everything, bringing famine and disease ... If the kings and nobles want to have wars, let them do the fighting themselves – but the working man should not get himself involved. While there is indeed no need for such good-for-nothings as monarchs and lords on this earth, war means a waste of hardworking and useful citizens.' 'Man ought not to kill his fellow man' – unless in self-defence. 'Wars will soon cease ... but one war still remains to be fought – a just war,' which will be waged 'according to God's will' against the oppressors of the people. 'It will be a war not of peasants against peasants, poor men against poor men, but of peasants against their lords, of poor men against the rich, of the oppressed and the wretched against the oppressors living in luxury ... On one side there will be arrayed Polish and Russian peasants and townsfolk and, on the other, the lords and kings, Polish and Russian. And peasants will shoot not against peasants but against lords.'

There are nevertheless members of the ruling class who are on the people's side: a few of the lesser gentry and officials and some of the lower clergy. These are not to be harmed but rather loved and respected for their stand.

The outcome of this great war of liberation which is approaching will be not only national independence but social justice:

After the war liberty, equality and fraternity will be established ... The land you cultivate will become yours; houses, barns, equipment, cattle ... will be yours ... You will not have to render labour services or to pay rents to your lords ... No one will be able to drive you from your fields or from your home ... You will have schools where your children will receive free education ... You will not have to give tithes to the priest nor pay him for baptisms or funerals or weddings.

In the meantime, the Letter warns the peasants, keep away from strong drink, which will only make you even poorer and stupider – 'until you have overthrown your enemies. After victory ... you will make merry.' Try to give your children some kind of education – your ignorance is one of the most effective weapons in the hands of your rulers. Above all, keep the Letter secret from those likely to be unsympathetic to the cause or betray it to the authorities – and do not give your lords any inkling of what is being prepared. If they get wind of the Letter's contents and order the clergy to attack it from the pulpit, take no heed. Those of you who help in spreading the good tidings will be granted an indulgence.

The Letter ends with the following exhortation: 'I expect, my beloved children, countryfolk and townspeople alike, that you will observe my counsels and teachings which I have given you here, and that you will quietly and obediently conform to the great change which will shortly come to pass to the glory of God and your own profit. Amen.'

The Letter did not enter into details as to how the new society was to be organized after the successful revolution. For further light on the opinions held by Ściegienny on the proper ordering of society we must turn to his later writings and to information given by fellow Poles who shared his exile in Siberia.[7]

The soil, in Ściegienny's view, was the common property of all men; and anyone trying to establish a claim to private ownership in it was infringing God's commandments.[8] Class differences should be a thing of the past; all capable of doing so should contribute their share of useful labour to the community. His guiding idea was that of labour ownership. Each commune *(gmina)* was to divide the land up equally among the peasants in individual holdings of thirty morgs apiece,[9] to be held on the basis of use. Giller notes Ściegienny's desire to balance in this way 'the natural desire for personal possession inborn in every man with the needs of the community and the ideals of communal ownership.'[10] Clearly there would be no room in such a scheme for the estates of a nobility that had lived for centuries off the labour of others; at the same time, with the land divided up equally among the able-bodied, the landless proletariat would disappear. The economic and social life of the village was to be directed by four elected officers whose business it would be to regulate such communal matters as the price of articles of consumption. Government was to be reduced to a minimum; there were to be few officials. Each village was to be equipped with a church and a school, where all children would receive a free education. The parish priest was assigned a leading role in social life: the religion of the community was to be based on the gospel ideals of brotherhood and equality.[11]

Thirty years later Ściegienny wrote: 'Profits from handicrafts, factories, commerce, and indeed from all industrial undertakings, are to go to a common treasury. The more this increases, the more taxes will decrease.'[12] But industry, and urban life in general, seem to have figured little in his scheme; nor does he appear to have thought out in detail the method by which the central organs of government would function. A hierarchy of representative institutions, from the communes at the base up to the central government, was to transform the country into 'a free commonwealth protected against the domination of an aristocracy, the selfishness of a plutocracy and the separate interests of individuals.'[13] On the international as well as the national level human society was to be infused throughout with the spirit of Christian equality and brotherhood.

Such, broadly, were the views which Ściegienny must have attempted to propagate among the peasants. In 1842 he had come into contact with members of the left wing of the underground Union of the Polish Nation (Związek Narodu Polskiego), consisting mostly of young men who, like Ściegienny, linked the winning of national independence with some vague form of social revolution.[14] The conspirators planned to start a new uprising in conjunction with the vicar, which would be centred on the Kielce-Lublin area. Ściegienny, though he continued to act independently, co-ordinated to some degree the activities of his peasant organization (Związek Chłopów, Union of Peasants, or, as Ściegienny himself called it, Towarzystwo Demokratyczne, Democratic Society) with those of the Union of the Polish Nation. In addition to his supporters among the peasantry, he was now assisted in his work in the countryside by a number of young revolutionary enthusiasts from the left wing of the Union. These, it should be noted, were almost all of gentry or middle-class origin, even though many of them – like the later Russian narodniks – had learnt a trade in order to gain more easily the confidence of the peasants among whom they carried on their work of revolutionary propaganda.[15]

In the summer of 1843, Ściegienny had moved from Wilkołaz to become parish priest in the village of Chodel, just outside Lublin. Early in 1844, a date was set for an uprising in the Kielce-Lublin area for the end of October. Feverish preparations were made during the next few months by Ściegienny and his friends. The conspirators at the last moment were prepared as a tactical move to compromise with their socialist principles. In order not to lose the support of the mass of the gentry for the coming uprising, they decided that landlords would receive compensation for the emancipation of their serfs.

By this time, however, the authorities, who had arrested a number of the leading members of the Union of the Polish Nation in the previous year, had already come upon Ściegienny's conspiracy. The vicar was apparently not a good organizer. Too much was left to chance, in the expectation that a mass uprising would carry everything before it. As a conspirator he was careless; he simply could not conceive that an informer would be found among his own peasants.[16] His naïve trust, however, was misplaced. On October 27, Ściegienny was arrested in Kielce, having been denounced to the authorities by a peasant who had attended a conspiratorial gathering addressed by him. The arrest of most of the vicar's associates, including his two brothers, followed shortly afterwards. After months of interrogation they were finally brought to trial and sentenced in May 1846. Ściegienny was condemned to deportation to Siberia for life, having first been deprived of his orders by his clerical superiors. The failure of the conspiracy did not destroy his faith in the social ideals he had hoped to realize by armed revolt. In Siberia he even tried to organize a 'phalanstery' among the other Polish prisoners – without much success. He remained in exile for a period of twenty-five years, until at the age of seventy-one he was granted an amnesty and returned to die nineteen years later in his native Lublin.

III

At the same period as Ściegienny was agitating among the peasants of his area on a platform of national independence and a vaguely drawn socialist Utopia, underground activity was also being carried on across the borders in the Prussian-occupied province of Poznania. Here Walenty Stefański[17] had created a secret society with a somewhat similar programme among the workers and small craftsmen, the shopkeepers and students of the provincial capital. Both men drew heavily for their ideas upon the writings of the émigré radicals and the French Utopian socialists; at the same time the framework within which they lived and worked – the loss of national independence and the social and economic conditions of the country – provided the motive force behind their action.

The son of a simple fisherman, Stefański was a printer and bookseller by trade, who succeeded in the course of time in gaining a modest competence through his business and, though with little formal education, a large fund of knowledge through his reading. He acquired a working knowledge of French as well as German, which helped to bring him into touch with the new social theories of the time. Stefański's father had reared his son in an atmosphere of patriotism, and when the uprising against the Russians broke out in the Congress Kingdom in 1830 the 18-year-old boy crossed the frontier to take part in the fighting. Later, towards the end of the 1830s, he settled in Poznań, where he set up his own printing establishment and bookshop. Little is known of Stefański's activities during these years. But by the early 1840s, like Ściegienny, he was already in contact with emissaries from the Poles abroad, mostly drawn from its radical wing; and he was instrumental in circulating the propaganda material they smuggled into the country. For this work Stefański, as a bookseller, was ideally placed. In 1842, in conjunction with several returned émigrés, he helped edit a popular paper *Postęp (Progress)*, which on account of the censorship had to be of an educational rather than a political character. Even so, permission to publish was withdrawn by the authorities in the following year. Already, on his own, Stefański had begun to organize the Polish artisans and craftsmen of the city of Poznań as a basis for a future uprising against the Prussian authorities. A few peasants from the surrounding countryside were drawn in too, as well as a number of apprentices, students, and older schoolboys who were formed into a separate youth section by two brothers, Leon and Maksymilian Rymarkiewicz. Among Stefański's closest collaborators in this work were the miller's apprentice Essman, the locksmith Lipiński, the waiter Andrzejewski, and the peasant brothers Palacz. The conspiracy thus had a petit-bourgeois, almost a proletarian, colouring, as is shown by the name chosen for it by Stefański: the Union of Plebeians (Związek Plebejuszy).

Stefański's earliest contacts with the emigration had been mainly with members of the centrist group which followed the historian Lelewel. The émigré party, however, which in the forties had most adherents in Poznania, was the left-wing Polish Democratic Society. The Society had set up a special committee in the capital, headed by the philosopher Karol Libelt and the historian Jędrzej Moraczewski. Both had been influenced by Lelewel's theories concerning the primitive Slav egalitarian commune as well as by the doctrines of the Saint-Simonians.[18] The Poznań Committee, despite its political radicalism, drew its main strength from the gentry and like the parent society was careful not to antagonize the class on whose support it reckoned most. Libelt and his friends were therefore proceeding very cautiously in their conspiratorial work. Collaboration between these upper-class nationalists and Stefański and his Union of Plebeians did not run smoothly. While in agreement with the democrats' committee in their patriotic aims, Stefański and his 'plebeians' accused its members of overdue caution and a lack of revolutionary ardour, if not downright cowardice, in attempting to postpone the date for the outbreak of the uprising as well as to limit its scope. 'It is the inactivity of the committee,' Stefański complained,[19] 'and its complete exclusion of artisans from participation in its work in which the whole people should rightfully share, that has caused him to act on his own.' Above all, the two groups differed on social questions.

The committee was strongly opposed to any attempt to curtail the property rights of the landowners by depriving them, even temporarily, of their manor farms. Stefański on the other hand, emphasizing the exploitation of the labouring masses in town and countryside, advocated a form of war communism, a socialist reorganization of agriculture, at least for the period of the insurrection.

Stefański himself left no record of his views on the future organization of society. But one of his opponents among the non-socialist democrats described Stefański's short-term programme in the following words: 'All personal property to be abolished for the time of the uprising and the administration of estates to be placed in the hands of the communes, so that the whole domestic economy, both private and public, be directed from above by the revolutionary government.' These ideas were regarded as 'quite impractical' by the majority of the Poznań committee and by the emissaries of the Polish Democratic Society who were working with it. The suspicion of 'socialism,' which would be aroused by 'a violation of the rights of property, even if only for the war period,' and the other radical demands put forward by Stefański's group, such as the right to work and equal pay, that suspicion might, it was further claimed, prove disastrous to the insurrectionary cause by setting against it the landowning class as a whole, and especially the reactionary squirearchy in neighbouring Galicia. However, Stefański's ideas met with considerable sympathy from several of the leaders of the committee's left wing. Moreover, a considerable influx of refugees from the Congress Kingdom, most of them young and hot-headed revolutionaries, had followed on the expiration in 1842 of Prussia's agreement to hand back to the Russians those attempting to flee across the borders. This new blood helped to radicalize opinion in Poznań.[20] Typical of such refugees was the fiery agitator Edward Dembowski,[21] who was in Poznania several times during this period and was in close contact with Stefański.

The breach with the committee remained unhealed. By 1845 Stefański's preparations for an uprising were nearing completion. The network of his conspiracy had by now come to include not only Poznania but also Pomerania and Upper Silesia.[22] But in the spring of 1845 arrests were made among the youth organization, and finally in November, as the result of information lodged with the Prussian police by a Polish nobleman, Count Maciej Mielżyński, Stefański and his leading associates were arrested too. For lack of proof of treasonable activities Stefański himself was acquitted in 1847 at a grand trial of Polish revolutionaries in Berlin. But although he was to remain active for many years in the independence movement, and his fierce antagonism towards the gentry was to continue unabated until his death in 1877, no more was heard from him of any new scheme for introducing a populist revolution during the period of emergency created by the outbreak of a national uprising.

Stefański's views on society may not have been shared in detail by all the members of his conspiracy. At the same time populist socialism had a small number of adherents in Poznań outside the ranks of the Union of Plebeians. Close ties probably linked all the populists, though there may have been minor differences of opinion. One of their number, Władysław Kosiński, writing a few years later when his radicalism had somewhat cooled, has described the basic ideas held in common.

The endowment of the peasantry with property rights *(uwłaszczenie)* is a foreign measure taken over from the enemy and not beneficial to the national cause. In such a division of the land they saw an undermining of the Slav commune *(gminna społeczność)*. It would give too great a preponderance to individualism and lead to a deterioration of the nation through awakening within it that materialism and fanatical attachment to property which, though as yet unknown [in Poland], has been so strong a mark of Western civilization. In a word, from a moral and patriotic standpoint they regarded the granting of property rights to the peasant as a disastrous measure. Instead they dreamt, therefore, of introducing a kind of social order more suitable to the national character, which would be based on brotherhood and some form of co-operation *(asocjacja)*.[23]

Kosiński goes on to give a fuller account of the views of one of the Poznań narodniks and a member of the left within the Poznań committee, Józef Mikorski. Mikorski, who had spent several years in France after the insurrection, became acquainted there with the ideas of the French Utopians. After returning home he gave visible expression to his radical opinions. Though he sprang from the country gentry and was himself the owner of a small estate, he adopted peasant dress and married the daughter of a village tavernkeeper.[24] Kosiński describes him as a man 'well known for his eccentricity but having some good ideas at times.' According to Mikorski:

In an uprising the nation must have at its disposal the whole strength and resources of the country. In a revolutionary struggle waged with the utmost effort private property will cease to exist almost of itself. Then government or army will become master of the whole national economy using it for the common needs of the country. The simplest thing would be, on the outbreak of the insurrection, to issue a proclamation that for the duration of the war private property is suspended and that the revolutionary government, as the expression of the nation's will, has by virtue of the revolution become the sole responsible steward of all the resources of the nation. It shall have the unquestioned right to conscript the population as well as to requisition money, grain, horses, cattle, no matter to whom they belong – with this proviso, that later, after the liberation of the country, payment or rather compensation shall be given in such fashion that the load will be adjusted according to income, so that no commune *(gmina)* or private individual will be overburdened. In every commune there shall be established an economic council elected by the vote of the whole community. This council will act, on the one hand, on behalf of the government as the lowest rung of the administrative hierarchy and, on the other, as the communal authority having charge of its whole economy, distributing according to its resources what is needed for the maintenance of each family and also apportioning the work fairly among all. During the revolution every good Pole must, from love of his fatherland and because of the exigencies of the moment, be content with the minimum essential to maintain life, with the expectation that all these sufferings and restrictions in satisfying their wants will one day be richly rewarded by the liberation of the Fatherland.

A commune which is unable to feed itself – for example, because war action has stripped it of its resources – shall apply to the neighbouring villages, or to more distant ones, for help. This should be given according to means and without reckoning or thought of repayment, simply from brotherly love, since everything on Polish soil belongs to the nation and is the common property of the whole. The community, therefore, owes to every individual at least enough to keep him alive.

Such a condition of evangelical communism *(ewangelicka wspólność),* which should be put into force by the communal councils (in which the village priest would be represented), will develop to the utmost feelings of equality, Christian love and brotherhood within the nation. And it is perfectly possible that this emergency revolutionary situation will appeal to the people and that, after the fighting is over, if the nation decides not to return to private ownership, it will be accepted by it and shaped into an organic system.

For us who only prepare for revolution such a question must be a matter of indifference. Let us not anticipate the will of the nation. Let the land return to its former owners, and be distributed to the landless merely when occasion presents itself. Or let village co-operatives *(asocjacje gminne)* be created. All this is not our concern. Let us confine ourselves to introducing the social structure appropriate to a revolution, that is, to suspending private property for the benefit of the nation.[25]

It is known that Mikorski was a member of the circle which existed in Poznań during the first half of the 1840s around *Tygodnik Literacki (The Literary Weekly),* edited by Antoni Woykowski in partnership with his talented wife, Julia.[26] The exact relationship between these intellectuals and the more plebeian group which looked to Stefański as its leader is unclear. But undoubtedly they shared many opinions in common.

The Woykowskis and their circle were strongly under the influence of the Western Utopians, particularly the Christian social democracy preached by such writers as Lamennais and Abbé Constant. They saw in Christianity a socially oriented creed and looked back hopefully to the primitive communism of the early church for a model for their own age. The restoration of a spirit of equality and brotherhood such as existed among the early Christians would mean a renewal of Christianity, a kind of second coming of Christ, whom they portrayed as the incarnation of human liberty revealing itself progressively in the history of mankind. The gospels they interpreted almost as social revolutionary documents. Official Catholicism was condemned for its betrayal of social Christianity and for its long alliance with political absolutism and aristocratic reaction. 'The religion of Christ and the democratic thought of today are only two aspects of one and the same system' wrote Kosiński.[27] In Julia Woykowska's view the true follower of Christ should renounce all his property. In one of her sketches Christ is depicted as a pilgrim wandering the earth with the dress he was wearing as his sole possession. 'I own nothing else on earth, and if you wish,' he tells a poor man, 'let us divide it up between us.'[28]

As with the other Polish narodniks both at home and in exile, it was the application of the new social theories to the peasant and the soil that occupied most of the attention of the Woykowskis' group: a reflection of the predominantly agrarian social structure of the Polish lands. The columns of the *Literary Weekly* were filled with denunciations of the landowning class and reflected sympathy, sometimes verging on the sentimental, for the victims of oppression. The gentry alone were held responsible for the peasants' social and cultural backwardness. A romantic idealization of peasant life was common to the whole group: among Julia Woykowska's most popular writings were her poems in the primitive style of authentic folk songs.[29] Ardent patriots and advocates of an imminent uprising, the Woykowskis did not believe, however, that the new and juster social order they dreamed of, when the land would be the common property of all who used it and men throughout the world would live together happily and virtuously in peace and harmony, could come through violent revolution. It would be brought about by the slow process of educating the people morally and intellectually and by gradual political enlightenment. 'Humanity makes progress but not by leaps' was how a member of the group defined their attitude.[30] The Woykowskis were not politicians, and though active in radical journalism until the end of the decade they exercised little influence on the Polish community in Poznań.

IV

Both Ściegienny and Stefański were men of action, practical revolutionaries rather than political theorists. Neither of them worked out detailed plans for the future socialist society, which they hoped would replace the old order on the achievement of national independence. On the other hand, the Woykowskis and their friends, who likewise failed to make an original contribution to social thought, tending for the most part passively to absorb the ideas of others, were intellectuals fearful of the possible consequences of social radicalism in action. In the person of Edward Dembowski[31] we have the man of action combined with the theorist – even though he too did not succeed during his brief life in creating a fully developed system.

Ściegienny and Stefański were both sons of the people. On the other hand, Dembowski, who was born in 1822, came from a wealthy aristocratic family. His father, who held high office in the government of the Congress Kingdom before the 1830 insurrection, had had his son educated at home, providing the boy with the best teachers available. The young Dembowski was especially interested in philosophy and literature, and it is with these subjects that much of his enormous literary output is concerned. In 1842, at the age of twenty, he started his own paper, *Przegląd Naukowy (The Scientific Review),* in Warsaw, providing out of his private income the money needed to cover the deficit on each issue and filling its pages mainly by his own pen. The new journal's earnestness and youthful enthusiasm, and a freshness of approach in strong contrast to the stuffiness and conservatism which was the dominant note in the Warsaw of the early 1840s, made its young and wealthy editor a welcome addition in the more progressive literary circles of the capital.

About this time Dembowski became associated with the work of the underground nationalist movement in the Congress Kingdom through his cousin Henryk Kamieński,[32] who had previously taken part in the insurrection. The cousins worked together in the Union of the Polish Nation with which, as we have seen, Father Ściegienny was also conected. The organization in Warsaw was composed largely of young artisans and apprentices, among whom vaguely socialist ideas were current; and through these contacts, as well as from his own reading, Dembowski's ideas on social problems quickly matured. When the conspiracy was partly uncovered by the Tsarist police in the summer of 1843, Dembowski, deeply implicated in the plans for a new uprising in the near future, was forced to flee across the border, escaping by way of Breslau to Poznań. Here, under the comparatively gentle Prussian régime, he was able to publish in the liberal Polish press articles openly expounding socialist doctrines. (He contributed to the Poznań *Literary Weekly* but soon broke with the Woykowskis whose brand of Christian populist socialism he regarded as too mild.) Here also he found a fruitful field of action in working with Stefański and his Union of Plebeians, on whose programme and organization he made a considerable imprint with his enormous energy and forceful personality. Meanwhile Dembowski was being closely watched by the Prussian police, and in the autumn of 1844 he was ordered out of the country. After a short time abroad, when he made personal contact with the leading left-wing émigrés, including Lelewel and members of the Democratic Society, Dembowski returned to Polish soil, this time to Austrian Galicia and in the capacity of an emissary delegated for conspiratorial work by the Democratic Society. For many months he wandered up and down the countryside, often in disguise, hiding at one time in a peasant's cottage, at another in the manor house of some radically inclined landowner, often narrowly escaping the attentions of the Austrian gendarmerie. His dynamic personality, full of revolutionary fire and romantic enthusiasm, his outstanding courage, and his calm in the face of danger became a legend. Regarded as a dangerous 'communist' by the Austrian authorities as well as by conservative Polish gentry, and suspect even to many of the liberal democrats as a firebrand who might succeed in turning the landowning class as a whole against their cause, Dembowski sought to arouse the peasant masses. In his view, it was the peasantry, not the gentry, who should constitute the main force on which to base the coming insurrection. Even so, he and his nearest associates refrained during this period from spreading revolutionary populist doctrines, merely promising that the insurrection would bring the abolition of serfdom to the peasant smallholders, who would receive the land they cultivated in unrestricted ownership, and some measure of land distribution to the rural proletariat.

The most revolutionary note perhaps was sounded by one of Dembowski's disciples, the equally youthful Julian Goslar,[33] who in 1845 composed an impassioned appeal *(odezwa)* to the peasants. Handwritten copies of the appeal, which was very similar in language and content to Ściegienny's Bull and probably to some degree modelled on it, were circulated in the villages by Goslar himself and the other young emissaries. 'To whom does the land for which you must perform labour services belong? Does it belong to the gentry or to the emperor, as they tell you? ... Villagers, your little plot of land belongs first of all to God – and then to him who tills it. It is through our own labours alone that we can acquire any of God's gifts.'[34] The practical programme of the revolutionaries, then, for all its socialistic undertones did not go beyond putting an end to serfdom and instituting independent peasant holdings, apparently permitting the gentry to retain their manor farms.[35]

In February 1846, the long-awaited uprising, which was originally planned for all three provinces, broke out in the Free City of Cracow. Dembowski played a leading part in the provisional government that was set up, doing his utmost to sustain its revolutionary enthusiasm. In its Manifesto of February 22,[36] granting the peasants their land and setting aside national property for the landless, the government went on in more general terms to call for the creation of a society 'in which each according to his deserts and his capabilities will be given access to the land,' where all privilege would be abolished and the young and the helpless taken under the state's special protection. Later the government would set up 'national workshops for craftsmen' – 'where the pay ... will be twice as high as they get today.'[37]

The speedy crushing of the uprising prevented this programme from being carried out. At the same time as the revolution was taking place in Cracow, the Galician peasantry, embittered by centuries of oppression and incited by the Austrian authorities, had risen in many districts against their Polish lords. Dembowski at once organized a procession from Cracow to win over the inflamed villagers for the revolutionary cause. The procession soon encountered Austrian troops, who began to fire, and Dembowski perished. He was in his twenty-fourth year.

Both in his theoretical writings on political and social problems and in his activity as an agitator Dembowski had been greatly influenced by his cousin Kamieński, while disagreeing with him on many important issues. Kamieński saw the fundamental cause of Poland's misfortunes in the landowning class's exploitation of their peasantry, who were consequently indifferent to the country's fate. He urged that a future uprising should be accompanied by a social revolution in which the peasantry would gain the land they tilled without compensating the landlords. At the same time Kamieński conceded the necessity of winning over the landowning gentry for the social as well as the political revolution. If they proved adamant in their opposition, however, 'terror' might be used as a temporary expedient not merely against individuals but against the gentry as a class. Like the Democratic Society, with whose work he was closely associated, Kamieński held that a more equal distribution of private property, not its abolition, was the most promising road to a more just society, and that in existing circumstances any attempt to introduce land nationalization would prove impracticable. While Stefański had advocated such a measure as one likely to win over the peasant masses for the national cause, Kamieński, more realistically perhaps, feared that it would be misunderstood by them and serve only to drive them into the arms of the partitioning powers. Kamieński was ready to admit that in a very thickly populated country where peasant land hunger was an urgent problem, where 'even small land-holdings begin to create a monopoly in relation to the mass of non-owners,' common ownership might prove the most suitable form of cultivation; but in a country like Poland with, as he claimed, land to spare for the landless, 'the minute parcellation of rural property is most desirable.' Only when, with the population continuing to rise, all the available land had been divided up – Kamieński never makes clear whether the estates of the gentry were to be available for this purpose – was there any need to consider nationalization of the land as a possible solution.[38] Kamieński, an admirer of the Saint-Simonians and Fourier, pictured a time when the slogan 'from each according to his capacities: to each according to his needs' would really be the community's guiding principle, but this would be in the far distant future.[39]

Kamieński's advocacy of terror as a weapon against the ruling class, his call for direct propaganda work among the peasantry, his setting an earlier date for the forthcoming insurrection than most of the émigré democrats were prepared to concede, and his linking of national independence with a solution of social problems became an integral part of Dembowski's political philosophy. When working among the Galician peasantry the latter did not step outside the programme of the Democratic Society, whose emissary he officially was, and he refrained during this period from openly preaching a radical transformation of society. As Kosiński writes: 'For the sake of harmony he sacrificed his personal viewpoint.'[40] Nonetheless Dembowski was far more of a social revolutionary than Kamieński or the other left-wing democrats.

Dembowski based his socialism on his view of history as a continuous progression from lower to higher forms of social life. Though influenced by Hegel, whom he at first regarded as his master, he was soon to reject the latter's deification of the existing order, and he was aided in reaching a new point of view by the works of Saint-Simon and his school, with their concept of social progress as the basis of change in history. Property relations altered as society took on new and higher forms: private ownership, therefore, was not a natural right.

According to Dembowski, following here his French models, the lowest stage of civilization is that of theocratic government, when private property has not yet appeared in any form. Man belongs body and soul to his priestly rulers. Next follows a period of absolute government in social and political affairs, though life is secularized and some freedom of thought exists. Common ownership of the means of production still prevails. The third stage is that of political despotism, when the ruler governs absolutely only in the political sphere. Society is by now divided into two classes: the privileged owners of hereditary private property and the unprivileged, who do not possess any property and have been reduced in many cases to slavery by the aristocracy. In the fourth stage this property-owning aristocracy takes over the reins of government, making the monarchy at first constitutional and then elective, and finally replacing it by republican forms. 'A constitutional monarchy,' Dembowski wrote, 'is a legalization of the privileges of the gentry and aristocracy. The people cease to be the immediate property of their lords, their slaves; their slavery nevertheless is no less burdensome, no less sanctified by the law. Man as such has in no way yet become a full member of society. Property bestows privilege and privilege constitutes citizenship.'

Only in the fifth stage, to be brought about by violent revolution, does political sovereignty lie with the people. Political democracy is now achieved, but social democracy, the final stage in the evolution of human society, has still to be reached. Only when social ownership of property and complete equality of educational opportunity are added to political democracy in its narrower meaning will the final goal be attained: 'a state of political, social and intellectual unity.'[41]

Before this 'gospel state of the peoples' (stan ewangeliczny ludów),[42] this 'absolute communism' (bezwzględna spólność)[43] as Dembowski calls it, can be realized, before the principle of love towards all men can predominate, exploitation of man by man in all its forms as well as all national hatred must be eliminated. In existing society, though personal violence and slavery have been rooted out in Europe at least, the enslavement of one nation by another, of one class by another, still continues. Its roots lie in private property, which makes the poor man dependent for his living on the rich. 'In the present state of the community he is only able to maintain himself when the rich man is graciously pleased to accept daily his grinding toil and to reward it after a fashion, since it is not the man who works but the man for whom he works, who fixes the pay.' The scales of justice in the state are likewise weighted against the poor man. Equality before the law is a fiction. In defence of their privileged position the wealthy do their best to prevent the poor from acquiring too much knowledge. 'And anyhow, how can those who, like the English working men, the French proletarians, and our dear and noble peasants, toil all the days and years of their lives, really develop their intellectual powers?'[44]

On only one occasion did Dembowski try to depict the ideal society of the future, and then but briefly. Drawing freely upon the ideas of the French Utopians, and of the Saint-Simonians, Fourier, and Proudhon in particular, Dembowski showed perhaps less originality here than in his analysis of contemporary conditions and of the historical process which served as a framework for his socialist theory.

In his ideal society all able-bodied persons would work under the direction of elected supervisors. There would be freedom of choice in the work done – except for the more disagreeable tasks, which would be performed by all on a rota system. Dembowski thought that no more than half the day at most would need to be devoted to labour; the remaining time could be spent on educational or recreational activity. No one might inherit any form of wealth. Here Dembowski criticized Fourier, whom he regarded as the most advanced social thinker of the time, for retaining inherited wealth in his schemes for establishing 'phalansteries' and for allowing private capitalists drawing unearned income on their shares to participate in the undertaking.[45] In Dembowski's view everyone should be entitled to use the resources of the community according to the social value of the labour contributed by him. An elected jury was to arbitrate in disputed cases. (Dembowski seems also to have envisaged a later stage in the development of society when distribution would be made solely on the basis of need.) Members of the community might live as they chose, either in separate houses or in a communal dwelling. The aged, the sick, and the young were to be provided for at the expense of the community. The village commune was to form the basic unit of government. The introduction of such a system in one nation, Dembowski optimistically thought, would lead inevitably to its acceptance in a short while by the rest of humanity.[46]

Dembowski left many details unfinished; contradictions may easily be detected in this scheme. But his main contribution to the development of social theory in Poland lies in the fact that he attempted to base his socialism on a scientific investigation of the laws of society rather than on a purely moral Utopia.[47] His premature death, however, prevented him from achieving all that his extraordinary talents promised.

V

In 1848, although the Congress Kingdom under the Russians remained in a state of uneasy quiet, revolution broke out both in Prussian-occupied Poznania and in Austrian Galicia. At this period industrial development in Poland was only in its infancy. In Poznania, for instance, only the capital Poznań and in Galicia only Cracow in the western half and Lvov in the east contained an artisan class of any size. It was composed for the most part of small independent craftsmen and their journeymen, and of petty shopkeepers; it was in no sense an industrial proletariat. The peasantry formed the overwhelming mass of the population. In the Russian and Austrian provinces, as we have seen, although in theory the peasants had been granted personal freedom, in practice that made little difference in their serf status since lack of industry gave them little possibility of escaping from their native villages. They were still forced as of old to do labour services on the land, in which they possessed no property rights. The manor house also enjoyed judicial and administrative rights over the villagers inherited from the Middle Ages.

In the Poland of 1848 the only forthright expression of agrarian socialist ideas came from an unexpected quarter, from one of its wealthiest landowners. There had been little in the previous career of Count Leon Rzewuski to indicate that he might come forward in 1848 as the standardbearer of socialism in the remote province of east Galicia, one of the most backward parts of the Austrian Empire.[48] By origin and education, and to a large extent in his personal ties, he was a member of the magnate class. The figure of the 'penitent nobleman' was not uncommon in Eastern Europe in the nineteenth century, and Poland, like Russia, provided many outstanding examples. But till 1848 Rzewuski had shown few indications of a tendency towards political radicalism, and little interest in politics at all. Yet in that year he became to his fellow landowners a symbol of subversive ideas, a dangerous 'communist' in the eyes of the class from which he sprang. In a few months he earned a reputation that the essential moderateness of his ideas and three subsequent decades of close collaboration with the conservative camp, begun in 1849, did not entirely succeed in effacing from the minds of his more reactionary fellow countrymen. Little wonder, then, that Stefan Kieniewicz has spoken of Rzewuski as 'a complicated and original figure, whom historians have found difficulty in deciphering.'[49] We shall deal with him here in some detail.

The Rzewuskis have left their mark on Polish history – sometimes gloriously, but not always. Leon's grandfather had been a leader of the aristocratic league known as the Confederation of Targowica, which in 1792 had called Russian troops into the country to defeat the constitutional reforms of the liberal party, thus precipitating the final partition of Poland. The ensuing disgrace to the family name was keenly felt by Leon throughout his life, and had fallen like a shadow over his father, an eccentric magnate who travelled widely throughout the Middle East dressed in Arab costume. Leon's mother, a charming and beautiful woman who was famous in her day as a society hostess, was perhaps the most formative influence on young Leon and on his elder brother, Stanisław, who was to be cut down in early manhood on the threshold of what promised to prove a brilliant career. A devout Catholic, she brought up her children in the principles of loyalty to the church and political legitimism. Both brothers, after studying in Vienna and Paris, had chosen a military career in the Congress Kingdom and served with distinction in the Polish army during the 1830-1 insurrection. During its last months Leon lost his only two brothers as well as his father, and he himself was forced to cross the border into Austrian territory. The Rzewuski estates were confiscated by the Tsar after the end of the uprising, but the family still held sufficient property in Austrian Galicia to keep it in the front rank of the landed aristocracy. Leon Rzewuski now settled in the ancestral castle at Podhorce in the eastern corner of Galicia. Apart from occasional visits to Cracow or Vienna and, from the early forties onwards, abroad in Italy, France, or England, Rzewuski remained in eastern Galicia; still a bachelor and to some extent a recluse, he seems to have spent most of his time in study, especially of history and political economy, and in supervising the family estate.

A special interest of his during those years was the breeding of horses, in which he became quite an expert, publishing a pamphlet on the subject. A cultivated country gentleman of considerable means, a collector of books and antiques, and an ardent researcher into family history, taking an intelligent interest in the affairs of the world but far removed from the realm of high politics, bearing also his share of responsibility in the obligations incumbent on a conscientious member of his class, yet not becoming too involved in local affairs, a lonely figure with more than a touch of aristocratic haughtiness who was regarded as something of an eccentric by his more philistine neighbours among the country gentry: this is the picture we gain of Rzewuski from scanty information during the thirties and early forties. Hostile to the methods and policies of the emigration, even of its conservative camp, though in sympathy with the ideal of national independence as a distant aim, Rzewuski, at least until the 1840s, when he was in his mid-thirties, does not seem to have shown at this time any sympathy with political or social radicalism. Certainly, during the insurrection he had been strongly opposed to all talk of social revolution, taking part in demonstrations which broke up left-wing gatherings.[50]

From early in the 1840s, however, a liberalization – it would be incorrect to talk of anything stronger at first – of his opinions on political and social matters took place. Increased travel abroad may have stimulated this gradual move leftwards, or perhaps it resulted rather from a deepening awareness of social problems given him by his studies and made real by his first-hand observations of peasant life in the surrounding countryside. The early spring of 1846 was to see a terrible rising of the Polish peasants in central Galicia (Rzewuski's neighbourhood, however, was not seriously affected). Then, urged on by the Austrian authorities, they plundered and murdered all landowners they could lay their hands on. Even the most obtuse among the ruling class could no longer ignore the problem. The discussions concerning peasant emancipation that since the beginning of the decade had been going on in the provincial Estates, a body dominated by the Polish landowners, took on a new urgency as the possibility of the central government forestalling the Poles became increasingly apparent. Far removed from the stubbornly reactionary outlook of too many of his fellow Galician landowners, who were eventually to let slip the opportunity now offered to win the peasants over by a generous gesture, Rzewuski possessed a sensitive and keen intellect which was acutely aware of his country's malaise.

The most vital problem in the world, he was writing in February 1846, just before the Galician massacre took place, is 'la question sociale qui est à la racine de tout.' Not absolute equality is what is needed, 'mais un besoin de justice. À chacun selon son mérite, et les chances pour tous,' he writes, echoing the Saint-Simonian doctrine.[51] By now he was quite familiar with the writings of the French Utopians and of Robert Owen, as well as those of the more orthodox English economists. He was in sympathy, he stated, with the aims of the Utopians but critical of the methods they proposed to reach the final goal. In his view they rated human virtue too highly so that their schemes, however excellent, were impractical. 'In dividing up material resources among the workers, some of them have destroyed property, the highest reward of labour; others by despotically directing production have destroyed liberty, that is, the natural development of capacities, while not giving immediately that moral and intellectual education which could fit men for such a state.' But in his view it was 'only in the presentation of their remedies that they were mistaken.' In their analysis and criticisms of the existing social and economic order there was much with which he could agree. 'It is certain,' he wrote, 'that a society ruled through competition will worship injustice so long as the workers are not in a condition to refuse too low wages in the same fashion as the owners are able to reject demands disadvantageous to themselves. This should be the task of a [proper] organization of labour, which has been vigorously proclaimed by the despairing workers of England as *a fair day's work for a fair day's wages.*' Unrestricted piling up of wealth should no longer be considered a nation's objective. Economics should be humanized, the emphasis put on distribution. 'The satisfaction of the needs of the greatest mass of people' should be 'the primary aim.' The country with the least number of persons in need will be considered the wealthiest, 'not the one which produces the most goods for exchange and the most capital.'[52] Rzewuski's visits to England, where he had seen the unhappy effects of unrestricted capitalism on the workers, and the influence of the English utilitarians were the obvious sources for the development of his ideas at this period.

Rzewuski's main concern, of course, lay with the peasants of his own Galicia. During the years immediately before 1848 he was active in trying to bring about a solution of the urgent problem of peasant emancipation *(uwłaszczenie)*[53] that would be acceptable to both peasants and landowners. The fall of Metternich, who had long played off Polish peasant against Polish landowner, in March 1848 opened the way for a reform of peasant relations throughout the Empire: the more enlightened Galician landowners now realized that labour services at least must be abolished and the peasants granted property rights in the lands they cultivated for their own use. Few agreed with the programme of the émigré democrats advocating that the landowners should not receive compensation for the financial losses they would suffer through emancipation. But some of the more progressive members of the landed class – Rzewuski among the first – did take the step of voluntarily emancipating the peasants on their estates, both as an act of conscience and as a gesture to encourage their fellow landowners.[54] And this also was the official policy of the Polish democrats. But on the whole the response was not good; the vast mass of the gentry feared the effect of the loss of unpaid peasant labour on their already shaky economic situation.

In this situation Rzewuski, in association with his cousin Adam Potocki, a future pillar of the Cracow conservatives, urged that the whole matter be considered at once by the provincial Estates. Realizing that to leave emancipation solely to the whim of individual landowners would be disastrous, they hoped that a collective decision might be quickly reached by the Poles themselves before the Austrian government had had time to impose emancipation from above.[55] Not only did Rzewuski and his cousin meet with opposition from the more reactionary landowners, but both men were branded by the democrats as themselves reactionaries – unjustly, since their object was to expedite, not to delay, a satisfactory decision.[56] Rzewuski's empirical attitude to politics and his disregard for a dogmatic approach contrasted with the more doctrinaire position of most of the Polish left, who objected to appealing to a body dominated by the landowning class. They disliked also the fact that Rzewuski and Potocki urged compensation to landowners if they lost the 'servitudes,' the rights to the forests and pastures disputed with the peasants; without compensation for these rights it would have been difficult at that date for large numbers of the smaller gentry to escape financial ruin. If Rzewuski's policy had been taken up energetically, emancipation might in fact have been enacted by the Poles; instead, on 22 April, before the provincial Estates had even met, the viceroy, Franz Stadion, issued an emancipation edict on his own initiative which was later confirmed by Vienna. Between the intransigence of the conservative gentry and the inflexibility of the Lvov democrats a great opportunity had slipped from the fingers of the Polish landowning class.

Rzewuski returned home in a pessimistic mood from conferences in Lvov with his fellow gentry in March and April. He confided to Potocki that

it seems more and more as if only the destruction of the old elements of the nation is coming to pass and not the blossoming of the nation itself. I cannot exclude from my thoughts the conviction that we live in an epoch such as there has not been since the period of the invasions of the barbarian peoples ... The former society passes ... I would be glad to depart for ever and bury myself in some quiet corner where the sky is blue and where the surge of the sea may be heard and where no yearnings penetrate ... The greater my trust in the future has been, the more I feel bitterness today! It is we who are throwing away the chance of a rebirth; it is we who are losing the friendship of the peoples as a result of our chauvinistic tendencies *(nienawistne dążności),* the good will of governments by our blind stirring up of disorder, and the sympathies of the friends of freedom by abuse of the democratic emblem![57]

This letter is important for an understanding of Rzewuski's thought. It expressed his disillusion with his own class and his feeling that it had outlived its usefulness; his fears that many of the values that in theory at least it had stood for were in danger of being lost along with its passing; his desire to achieve a common platform with the other peoples living alongside the Poles, in particular with the Ukrainians of east Galicia among whom national consciousness was beginning to stir; and finally his anxiety to combine social and economic justice with political stability. All these characteristic elements are to emerge in greater fulness in his series of pronouncements on political and social questions during the year of revolution.

Rzewuski indeed was not to depart for his desert island. The new political situation in Galicia, as in the other Austrian lands, resulting from the March revolution in Vienna led to a temporary relaxation of the official press censorship and to a considerable degree of political freedom. New journals were begun and old ones took on new life.[58] A number of émigrés returned to serve on the editorial staffs of the radical press. Every shade of Polish opinion from ultra-conservative to left-wing democrat was represented, and in addition there were the papers of the Ukrainian groups and an official government press. In only one quarter, however, were socialist – agrarian socialist – views consistently expressed, and that was in the articles contributed by Rzewuski to one of the newly founded journals, *Postęp (Progress).*[59]

Shortly before leaving Lvov he had taken part in setting up the paper, probably providing the main financial support for a venture that was not likely to be able to pay its way at the beginning. The first number appeared on 15 April. Its four-page issues came out three times a week: on Tuesdays, Thursdays, and Saturdays. From time to time a special supplement was also published. The editorship was shared by two young men, both still in their twenties: Karol Widman, the Polonized son of a German settler in Galicia, and Jan Zacharyjasiewicz, who had already spent several years in an Austrian prison. They had not had much journalistic experience, but they were enthusiastic democrats. Rzewuski was not officially connected with the paper, and editorial comment occasionally took issue with him on some topic. Nevertheless it would seem that Rzewuski, some twenty years older than the official editors and with the prestige that his wealth and social position gave him, exercised at first a deciding influence on the paper's policy.

The paper's programme was formulated in an editorial in the first issue. The editors would seek to spread the idea that all the country's inhabitants should be considered citizens with equal rights. All were equally members of the nation, whether peasant, craftsman, or landowner. In addition, the interests of humanity came before those of nations. These were the principles in the light of which they would judge the laws and administration of the country.[60] In subsequent issues the paper came out strongly in favour of far-reaching political democracy; it showed itself strongly anti-gentry and was inclined to idealize the peasantry as the basis of society; it stood for international co-operation between states, the brotherhood of the Slav nations, and the federative principle for the peoples who made up the former Polish commonwealth. It was decidedly opposed to the chauvinism of the Polish right wing, pleading for equal rights for the Ukrainians and the Jews alongside the Polish population. It printed a number of translations from the French socialist press, including the writings of Louis Blanc and those of Fourier and his disciples.[61] But if we ignore Rzewuski's own contributions it did not officially advocate any form of socialism. Though *Progress* certainly belonged to the left wing of the democratic camp, its editors and contributors, like almost all the other Polish political radicals of '48, did not share the extreme social radicalism of their aristocratic colleague.

During the brief four and one-half months of the journal's existence Rzewuski contributed to *Progress* some thirty-five short articles written in a pithy, aphoristic style. Four themes run like a refrain through the whole series: the passing of the gentry's role as the leader of society; the need for radical social reform, for replacing the existing order by 'socialism'; the relationship of political democracy to constitutional changes; and finally the problem of nationalism, of the place of Poland among the Slav peoples and within the international community of nations.

According to Rzewuski, the origins of the privileged position of the aristocracy and gentry lay in their role in the Middle Ages as leaders of the community in war and peace. 'The power of the aristocracy was based on its usefulness.' Later, real authority passed into different hands: it became vested in the monarch or in other classes of society. 'The mission of the aristocracy came to an end.' Today in Poland the landowning class still preserves, as if by inborn right, its privileged position in politics and social relations but, with a few honourable exceptions, it does nothing to deserve this by any equivalent services. As a result it has become increasingly divorced from the rest of the nation, more and more unpopular with the mass of the people. The peasants make no distinction in this respect between the aristocratic owner of vast estates and the small gentleman with his one manor; all are members of a ruling caste, divided by a gulf from the people. Until now the historic Polish nation had been a Poland of the gentry – 'for ourselves we respect historic national feelings but we do not see how this 'nationality' would be able to create anything permanent for the fatherland.' Respect for the national tradition, which should be dissociated from all connection with aristocratic exclusiveness, must be engendered among the people; their national consciousness, still dormant today, must be awakened. Rzewuski appealed to his fellow landowners in the following words:

Throw off, therefore, the guise which brings hatred upon you. Concern yourselves in all sincerity with the people's lot. Take the lead in the struggle for progress, as your forefathers led in battle. Stand at the head of the people as they surge forward towards enlightenment and freedom, and strive after distinction only by your greater enthusiasm. If you will not do this, if you will not break away [i.e. from your past], they will forget you. If, however, you determine on hostility, you will perish.

If the gentry would not abandon their class exclusiveness they must be considered 'an obstacle to the most sacred cause of the democratic rebirth of the fatherland. We will not cease from repeating: ego autem censeo delendam esse Cartaginem.' Accused of treachery to his own kith and kin, even of advocating the physical destruction of the ruling class, he replied: 'Be what you want, gentlemen, in your social habits, be models of culture, live according to your hearts. Such liberty cannot be denied you. But to be a political caste? To remain an aristocracy?' To this he was unalterably opposed; for this there was no place in a constitutional state acknowledging 'the sovereignty of the nation (udzielność narodu).' A hereditary noble 'estate,' in the sense of a privileged order, was incompatible with political equality. It was inseparably bound up with the principle of absolute government. 'Hence we deduce that the noble class, however well-meaning, must, after the fall of absolutism, go over sooner or later to a reactionary position.'[62] It was for this reason, therefore, that Rzewuski strongly criticized the ultra-conservatives of east Galicia, who early in May had set up a Landowners' Association in Lvov in opposition to the National Council. The latter grouped together the more liberal among the Polish gentry alongside the middle-class democrats. The Landowners' Association on the other hand represented the interests of the owners of the large estates, and although it was reluctantly prepared to acknowledge the abolition of serfdom as a fait accompli it aimed at maintaining an unchallenged ascendancy of the landed class in the countryside and the old patriarchal relationship between manor house and village.[63] No good could come of such action, Rzewuski stated: the attempt to defend à l'outrance the exclusive position of 'a caste, an aristocracy of property,' would only succeed in arousing among the people a hatred even more bitter than already existed.[64]

Rzewuski, however, went further than the democrats of the Lvov National Council – or than the editorial board of his own paper – in his understanding of the implications of that 'sovereignty of the nation' which should replace sooner or later both monarchical absolutism and the dominant social position of the landed class. For the principle on which the new political and social order was to be built Rzewuski uses the term socialism. Here is what he meant:

Socialism is a philosophy of social principles recognizing the sovereignty of the nation in economic relations as well as in political life. It does not single out any fraction of humanity as its aim; it does not choose for its foundation any historical legends or memories. In its theory it is guided by absolute truth; in its practice it starts from the actual situation and, striving towards the realization of its principles, it at the same time renounces inflexibility of action. Being indeed a democratic and revolutionary doctrine, socialism has been hated by the majority of those who have preserved a filial respect for the past or have a possessor's adoration for the conditions resulting from the past. Socialism in fact is democratic in so far as it aims at the prosperity of the whole without regard for separate classes ... Socialism is revolutionary, too, in that it rejects the principle of authority, summoning every edict to answer before the court of reason and conscience. However, in action it does not wish to use revolutionary means, it does not want to rule mankind through violence; it desires instead to enlighten and to convince, regarding education as the essential condition for material progress.

He goes on to describe socialism as 'the idea of humanity,' 'the science of applying the gospels to the needs of this world.' It is anti-individualist and therefore hated by all whose profits it threatens. The 'apostles of socialism,' he says, must be ready to sacrifice everything and face unpopularity on all sides for the sake of their beliefs.[65]

In the French Revolution the Third Estate had won political equality with the former privileged orders. The new political doctrine that achieved this was known as liberalism. 'Today the people, that is, the class of manual workers, is demanding – and with reason – its right to a just reward for its labour. The theory which is occupied with this question is called socialism.' Not long ago liberalism was regarded as subversive and the enemy of religion; now it is quite respectable. Similarly a time would come when socialism would seem mild. Rzewuski failed to comprehend how true democrats could be anti-socialist. Socialism is merely 'a practical application of democracy to the life of the people'; it is 'economic democracy,' since 'having granted political rights to the people you must give them the possibility of using them.' 'We see in the same ranks the enemies of democracy and the enemies of socialism. Whoever upholds political democracy and does not want socialism, either does not understand the meaning of democracy or desires to use it deceitfully for dirty ends.' Every member of society must be assured the right to work and should be given the instruments of labour, the tools and raw materials by which he can maintain himself and produce for the good of society as a whole. This was no visionary Utopia like the schemes of Fourier and Cabet, Rzewuski claimed, it was merely what may be deduced from the writings of professional economists such as Adam Smith or Ricardo, Bastiat or Sismondi. Socialism, in his understanding, did not signify the establishment of a perfect world, an end to all human suffering and discontent. What is needed to ameliorate distress, he went on, is 'high moral culture: love in the rich, suffering in the poor. This is what the gospels teach us; in this socialism consists.'[66] Socialism in fact is simply 'the political expression of the teaching of the gospels, the social Messiah whose rule the Christian world calls for daily in the Lord's Prayer.'[67]

In regard to property, the central issue in all discussions of socialism in Rzewuski's day as in ours, he puts forward a concept of labour ownership. Only labour can create individual property rights; they can arise only as 'a reward for work.' Where no human labour has been contributed, men have a natural and God-given right freely to enjoy the products of the earth. But since all men possess a right to develop their own powers to the utmost, provided they do not harm other members of the com-

munity, then with the unequal capacities of different men, which Rzewuski postulates, inequalities in the products obtained by labour must arise: 'Equality in unhindered activity has been the basis of inequality in
possessing ... Inequality of possessions is thus founded on the principle
of social equality, since it is the result of an unequal output of labour.' A
'social equality,' therefore, or as he also calls it 'the universal law of social brotherhood, which presupposes full equality of opportunity in acquiring property through labour, is not a principle subversive of property but rather one establishing it on a firm rational basis. 'Socialists
maintain that the aim of a community is the good of all; individual talents, skill and riches ... must ... be subordinate to the common welfare.'
Therefore, by emphasizing the social utility of property when used properly in the interests of the community, they provide a better apology for
it than its so-called defenders, who seek blindly to vindicate the whole
existing order. Social equality, or socialism, is different, and indeed more
important than equality of political rights. Sometimes it may even appear in conflict with the latter, for 'social equality grants an equal right
of raising one's self in practice over others by one's own efforts – provided only that one remains obedient to the moral sovereignty of the
whole community and justifies one's superiority by services to it.'

Rzewuski did not consider the immediate application of his ideas on
social equality to be within the realm of practical politics, although he
was convinced of their ultimate triumph.[68] Moreover, while his principles were quite consistent with individual peasant cultivation it would
be difficult to square them with the retention by the gentry of the manor
lands, which the Polish democrats were prepared to acquiesce in for the
sake of national solidarity. Yet his writings show no sign that he ever
contemplated the introduction of a *Loi agraire* which would redistribute
the estates of the landed class among the peasantry. And on the difficult
question of the inheritance of property Rzewuski always remained
silent.

Communism of goods, as in the theories of Cabet and his school, or
even in the milder Fourierist guise of phalansteries, Rzewuski considered a Utopian fantasy incapable of realization within the forseeable future. He did not regard it with the horror with which it was greeted in
most quarters but stressed the peaceable character that its proponents
gave it. It was for him an honest attempt to find a solution to some of
the most urgent problems of the day, an idea that had nothing in common with the anarchic violence with which its enemies sought to confuse
it. Anyhow, there was no need to fear communistic theories would take

root in a country like Galicia – once the peasants had been given their land.

Rzewuski was at one with almost all the French Utopians in opposing social violence; as with the Saint-Simonians or Fourier, for instance, there was no place in his schemes for any doctrine of class struggle. There he parted company decisively with most of the other early Polish socialists, whether in the home country or in the emigration, who, for all their emphasis on the peasantry and the agrarian structure, held fast to the *babouviste* tradition of class warfare as a basis of their socialist creed. 'A uniting of the classes is the first condition for the rebirth of the fatherland,' Rzewuski wrote.[69] In another place he said: 'We would have no part in any revolution; we do not feel any calling to change the principles of the state. If these principles are opposed to ours, then we withdraw from all collaboration; if they are in conformity with ours, we profit from the existing liberties; but in any case we submit to the principles which the community has accepted.'[70] Not that he did not observe social struggle in the world around him: that would have been a difficult feat in the year 1848. After the 'June Days' in Paris he wrote:

The bloody struggle between capital and labour in the streets of Paris has proved how great is the need to put an end to the industrial anarchy which goes by the name of free competition. Liberty is a lie where the worker must either bow to the will of the capitalists or die of hunger. On the other hand, however, the capitalist also is often forced to succumb to the pressure of the market in measuring the reward of labour ... To defend the workers from the greed of the capitalists, and the latter from the unjustified demands of their workers, is essential. A legal right of supervision over private industry belongs undoubtedly to the community. Courts, therefore, should be set up to which workers and capitalists alike could take their disputes. The principles according to which labour should be rewarded, and the competence of the courts, must be defined. In this way a solution of this most important question will be found.[71]

In places he put forward an almost Hegelian view of the role of social conflict in history. Both the old and the new are necessary, he urged. The ancien régime is now represented chiefly by Russia; the new forces in society are those released by the French Revolution. From the clash of these two principles in every nation there had resulted the forward march of civilization. In the last issue of *Progress* Rzewuski wrote that conservatism, provided it was not simply a blind, unthinking opposition to everything new, might have a positive function to fulfil in bringing about a new social order. It could cause 'a slowing down only in the movement, which will be of benefit to the nation.' This would give ideas and theories time to ripen, to be adjusted to political reality; such delay would also ease the transition and cause less damage to society than a violent revolution. 'We assert that, although the conservative parties take upon themselves a great responsibility [i.e. for resisting change], yet they are as necessary to the progressive movement as are liberal oppositions in the case of conservative governments.' In this way hostile forces might be harmonized, and as violent passions slowly subsided, the idea of universal brotherhood would cease to be a Utopian dream.[72] For Rzewuski, therefore, socialism would not result from destruction of the existing structure of society but rather from a merging of the two opposing patterns in a higher form.

Equality was indivisible, even if social equality, or socialism, was ultimately more basic than political equality, or democracy. Nevertheless Rzewuski devoted more attention to the preconditions for establishing political democracy as the most immediately practicable goal, thus revealing the essentially reformist, almost Fabian, character of Rzewuski's political ideas. He was not primarily interested in the nature of the political régime: 'It is the goal of action and the source of power that is the mark of democracy. The aim of democratic government is the good of the greatest number,' not class interests. Democratic forms could also provide 'a ladder for individuals to climb to absolute power in the state.'[73] Freedom of the press and of assembly, guaranteed personal liberties and far-reaching provincial autonomy, parliamentary institutions: these were better safeguards for political democracy in existing circumstances than universal suffrage.[74] 'One man one vote' was excellent in principle and a slogan that might be possible to implement immediately in the towns.

But the village folk living at great distances from each other, for whom the domestic holding is much dearer than any labours connected with a constitution, would never want to lose working days, and to travel far afield, in order to vote directly for deputies at a gathering of whose workings they had little conception ... Therefore, I will never regard as friends of the people those who wish to impose direct voting at the elections on the whole mass of the people. By universal but indirect suffrage taking place in the communes in proportion to the population, respect is paid to the equality and self-government of the nation and, in our opinion, consideration had, too, for the thoughts, needs, and customs of the rural labouring class.

Political machinery alone would not guarantee democracy. Freedom has meaning only if we know how to make proper use of it. As with so many reformers from the eighteenth century onwards, education was Rzewuski's panacea for the ills of the state: 'The degree of freedom is in particular dependent upon the level of education.' The freest countries in the world were those like England, France, or the United States, where education was spread most widely.[75]

Rzewuski's attitude on the suffrage question, first stated in one of his leaflets issued in association with Potocki at the end of March,[76] contrasted with his radicalism on other issues.[77] It was criticized at the time by a writer in Rzewuski's own *Progress,* who detected in Rzewuski's proposals for limiting direct voting to the educated and financially independent sections of the community what this writer described as 'the establishment of the influence of the old magnate class.'[78] Rzewuski replied that such had not been his purpose at all; he merely wanted 'to secure representation in a single House, not for birth, but for large landed property, the acquisition of which, he added somewhat naïvely, was now 'accessible to all.' 'There is certainly a strong trend against bigger properties'; his object had been to assure their owners a representation in the legislature proportionate to their present importance for the country.[79] This restriction of the peasants' voting rights was for Rzewuski clearly a temporary measure until education had become more general in the countryside. Whatever his doubts about its immediate application, the principle of universal suffrage was a valid one he believed, and he disapproved of the attitude which had led to the direct vote being given in the June elections in Galicia only to the gentry and the middle class, a chauvinistic spirit present even among the Polish democrats, who were fearful of the Polish and Ukrainian peasants' reactions to the national appeal. 'Such considerations,' he wrote, 'could not find favour with radical socialism, since socialism is not directed at Polish nationality but at the development of the people.'[80] (The arch-revolutionary Blanqui likewise took up a negative attitude towards an immediate grant of universal suffrage to the masses. Moreover, in 1848 universal suffrage gave an electoral majority to the conservative peasantry and thus brought on a European-wide reaction against the revolutionary movement and finally its defeat.)

In his rights as a citizen the peasant must be on an equality with his former master. On this basis the disdain on the one side and the suspicion on the other would die away as relations ceased to be those between inferior and superior. Rzewuski pleaded:

If the gentry will only act with intelligence, having perceived the unity of their interests with those of the village commune *(gromada)*; if they will recognize in the peasant a man with his own pride and feelings, and not merely a [part of the] labour force; if they will only turn their higher level of education to enlightening their brothers; then, having become benefactors of the people, they will undoubtedly become, in the best sense of the word, leaders of the communes. In raising up the people to the dignity of the nation they will be bestowing very great benefits on the nation, and they will discover that to lead the people is the most honourable calling there is.[81]

What needed to be done to bring about this union of interests? In his answer to this question lay the kernel of Rzewuski's political philosophy, his solution to the riddle of how to combine the principle of democracy with the existence in practice of a politically and culturally backward electorate: 'The truly democratic principle insists above all on securing self-government for the village communes.' Here at the grass roots, beginning with village institutions and working upwards, was the social reformer's proper sphere of action. Rzewuski quoted the two-volume work published in the previous year by Baron von Haxthausen, whose views on the peasant commune in Russia were to exercise such an influence on Herzen and the Russian narodnik movement. Rzewuski wrote:

The commune (in Russia the *mir*) is a living element in Slavdom, and being a pure form of democracy it assures the Slavs strength in the future. But this element is not bureaucratic *(biurowładczy)*, therefore it has either been forgotten or deliberately ignored ... The commune is the peasants' fatherland. There he can develop freedom, love, brotherhood and order, and create a foundation for the national life by associations between one commune and another ... At this time, when the spirit of association has embraced the community, we need to preserve carefully the communal associations – a concept both national and peculiar to the Slavonic race *(szczep)*, and the political expression, too, of brotherhood.[82]

Let gentry landowner and peasant smallholder meet together in the commune and work there for the common good. 'In a political sense the gentry no longer exists, for every citizen is linked together in the commune where he has his legal domicile. But so long as one gentleman landowner makes common cause with another, you have a caste.'[83] Rzewuski ignored the fact that among his countrymen the communistic tradition preserved among the Russian peasantry was absent. (This fact was also ignored by most of the other Polish protagonists of the peasant commune, whether of the conservative right or of the left wing, beginning with Lelewel, from whose historical works they drew a large part of their inspiration.) Rzewuski shared with the later Russian narodniks their idealization of the peasant. 'The Polish peasant,' he wrote, was 'the soundest and the strongest element of the nation, outliving all upheavals and changes and preserving what the other strata have misused.' A friend of Rzewuski's speaks of 'the astonishing regard he had for the peasant estate,' of how his aristocratic aloofness disappeared in meeting members of the peasantry and was replaced by a feeling of respect for the human being.[84] Time and again Rzewuski's thinking was to return to the village commune in whose development he saw the political and social salvation of the nation. In 1848 he styled himself 'citizen of the commune of Podhorce,'[85] the village where he had his castle! He was still discussing the commune's problems publicly and privately at the end of the year (by which time he had become thoroughly disillusioned with the chances of bringing about far-reaching social reforms in the Galician environment); it was the subject which occupied him most at the time of his death twenty-one years later, long after he had severed all connection with movements that might be termed socialist or radical. In the commune alone did he see, in 1869 as in 1848, a secure foundation for a just social order.

In Rzewuski's pronouncements on the village commune, given above, we may detect an element of Slav Messianism, of the idea of the peculiar mission of Poland within the community of Slav nations. Certainly the writings of Mazzini were an influence on Rzewuski here, as they had been on other thinkers of the Polish left. Poland, says Rzewuski, occupies the same position within Slavdom as France does within Europe; it is the mission of the Polish nation to lead their brother Slavs towards a new and freer political and social order. 'Poland is the expression of the principle of liberty within Slavdom.'[86] But, as with Mazzini, the idea of national mission was united with a doctrine of internationalism, of a harmony of separate national interests within the international community. Rzewuski tried, not altogether with success, to define what he meant by nationality. A nation, he asserted, is made up of all those who share a common territory and language. 'The intellectual tie of language maintains national unity when political circumstances have broken the ties of common habitation.' The concept of nationality which flows from this community of interests may change its external forms 'according to the spirit of the epoch.' 'When realization of nationality is to be found in a minority of a nation, this minority represents the nation and masters it by the strength of its idea.' It has an obligation to arouse a feeling of national self-consciousness in the masses. This political awakening of the folk will result at first in a feeling of hostility towards the national élite, since the former now feels its own strength and at the same time senses the differences between the two strata without comprehending their common foundations. The national élite must do its utmost to break down such suspicions by the spread of knowledge and enlightenment, by disseminating the gospel of 'liberty, equality and fraternity,' without however trying to impose on the people forms alien to their previous experience and traditions. 'Only with enlightenment and the realization of its own strength will the people arrive at national feeling.' But 'knowledge must precede baptism.'[87]

What, in Rzewuski's view, should be the relationship between populism and nationalism? The old nationalism based on the historic claims of a privileged ruling class, he wrote, must be rejected out of hand. A concept based upon a natural conflict of interests between nations ought likewise to be ruled out. A populist theory of nationalism must realize that the feeling of nationality is a fact. 'We however, while respecting "nationalisms" like all other forms in which the development of humanity clothes itself for a time, presume that they are only passing shapes.' At this particular stage of history they fulfil the function of 'joining families into a greater whole and destroying the absolute individuality' of smaller groups now brought together into a larger unity. But national consciousness does not constitute an essential element in human nature. It is in any case subordinate to the needs of humanity.[88]

Rzewuski devoted much attention to the application of theory to the practical situation existing in Galicia. In fact all his articles on the national question during this year were written with one eye to the political reality. How were conflicting demands of Polish and Ukrainian nationalists, the one representing historical and the other ethnic claims, to be brought into some kind of harmony? This was the main question to which Rzewuski sought an answer. The first step, in his view, was to broaden the concept of Polish nationality. He distinguished between the idea of the old historic Poland, which the ruling class still clung to, and that of a 'people's Poland,' which held the promise of the future. 'All efforts aiming at the destruction of the historic element have made it easier for popular "nationality" to reach self-sufficiency and have made it conscious of itself. To observe this must please the far-sighted, since it is from this "nationality" that a new Poland can arise and never from memories of the past.' The masses had demonstrated their opposition to the old Poland of the gentry by their loyalty to the Habsburg Emperor and to the Austrian bureaucracy. Indeed, what greater proof was there of the existence within Galicia of these 'two nationalities' (as he called them), gentry and peasantry, than the fact that in the eastern part of the province separatist tendencies had already arisen among the Ruthenian intelligentsia and peasantry?

If we want to avoid the destructive action of the people's 'nationality,' let us not attempt to oppose it; on the contrary, let us put ourselves at its head ... Let us welcome the Poland of the future, the people's Poland. Let us not raise up the sacred shades of the old Poland of the gentry. We should preserve our respect for it in our hearts, while imitating the virtues of the old Poland in framing the new ... [But] today we can have no other thought except to educate and raise up the people's 'nationality' and to throw in our lot with it without reservation.

The immediate reaction of the Polish community to early expressions of Ukrainian nationalism had been mainly one of surprised hostility. The Ruthenians, as the Ukrainians of east Galicia were then called,[89] were usually regarded as one out of a number of ethnic groups making up the Polish nation; their language was considered to be a dialect of Polish. There was no difference on this question between conservatives and democrats. None were more insistent than the latter in calling for a restoration of Polish independence within the boundaries of the 1772 frontiers. The attempt to make of the Ruthenians a quite separate nationality was considered a manœuvre of either Austrian bureaucrats or Tsarist agents to sow dissension in the Polish camp; and in fact the most vocal element among the Ukrainians at this period was the conservative group headed by the upper Uniat clergy, who were strongly pro-Austrian and anti-Polish. As yet a consciousness of Ukrainian nationality among the Ruthenian peasantry was even weaker than national consciousness in the Polish village.

Certainly the Polish democrats in 1848 demanded equal rights for the Ruthenians as for the Poles proper. But, they also refused to recognize the existence of an independent Ukrainian nationality.[90] Among his contemporaries, and indeed for some decades to come, Rzewuski was alone among the Poles in his readiness to acknowledge the right of the Ruthenians in Galicia to separate from the Poles and to form, if they wished, an independent nation. For this of course he was bitterly attacked by all parties among his fellow countrymen, who accused him of betraying national interests. Galicia was an artificial creation of the partitioning powers, Rzewuski answered. Let the province then be divided into two parts, the Polish and the Ruthenian. If the latter wished to enter into a union with the Poles in the event of Poland's regaining independence, no one would be more happy than Rzewuski. Indeed he believed that such in fact would be the outcome of allowing the Ruthenians a completely free development. The influence among them of the clerical and pro-Austrian party, which he disliked intensely, would then disappear, and the Ruthenians instead would tend to follow the lead given by the more culturally advanced Poles. 'Poland is the highest grade in Slavdom; the Ruthenians the most elementary. Every effort, therefore, made to raise the [Ruthenian] people in education will bring them nearer to us.' The two nations were so akin to each other as almost to constitute a single whole. Nevertheless, 'if Ruthenian nationality really exists,' and this of course he was ready to grant, 'then by this very fact it has a right to independence like every other nation. If, on the other hand, it is only fabricated, spurious, its independence will not amount to more than that of any other part of Poland.'[91] Here none of Rzewuski's contemporaries, however radical, were prepared to follow him, not even his own paper, *Progress,* which rejected any scheme to relinquish part of Polish territory by separating the Ruthenian from the Polish districts of Galicia.

Rzewuski's defence of the national rights of the Ukrainians, as well as his views on the reorganization of society, brought a chorus of angry criticism from all sides. His chief antagonist was the organ of the Landowners' Association, *Polska*. Its editor, a former liberal turned reactionary, Hilary Meciszewski, accused Rzewuski of stirring up hatred between one class and another, of a lack of patriotism, and of trying to provoke civil war. His views, subversive of all good government and indeed of society in general, were 'false and dangerous.'[92] Similar attacks appeared in other sections of the press and in the pamphlet literature of the day.[93]

With the editors of *Progress* Rzewuski, as we have seen, was not altogether at one either in his views on socialism or in his attitude towards the Ruthenian question. At the end of August the paper closed down, and though a new journal *(Gazeta Powszechna)* replaced it under a broadened editorial board which included Widman and Zacharyjasiewicz, Rzewuski after the first few weeks no longer figured as a contributor. We do not know the exact reasons for his withdrawal, but they were probably connected with the differences of policy which had already been revealed.[94] However, the days of a free press in Galicia were almost over; in November the officer in command of the imperial forces, General Hammerstein, bombarded Lvov; and with the city's occupation by Austrian troops ended the brief period of liberalism. The small headway Rzewuski had been able to make in favour of his views, the stubborness and blindness of so many of his fellow countrymen from the gentry, and the narrow nationalism of the bourgeois democrats had by the autumn left him a thoroughly disappointed man. 'La scission actuelle entre Ruthènes et Polonais,' he writes, 'pourrait en ce moment être terminée ou du moins mitigée, si l'on avait la possibilité de contenir l'immense majorité d'imbéciles qui nous déborde.' However, he reports, 'mon extrême impopularité dans un certain parti me procure une position avantageuse pour ces affaires-là et la bienveillance du peuple dans le district me renforce.' With some bitterness he contrasts the confidence shown to him by his Ukrainian villagers with the opposition of the middle-class Polish democrats in the National Council, who had been saying 'que je veux me faire Vladique!'[95]

His activities during the preceding months are summed up in a letter he wrote at the end of the year to a Belgian friend:

J'apprends par une lettre de Bruxelles qu'une calomnie lancée contre moi dans mon pays a trouvé des échos parmi mes compatriotes à B[ruxelles] et je suppose qu'elle sera arrivée jusqu'à vous ... Il est nécessaire que je vous explique les causes de ces calomnies stupides. Notre *gentry* s'est conduite depuis le mois de mars de la manière la plus fatale aux intérêts de ma patrie. Turbulante vis-à-vis du gouvernement, méprisante envers le peuple, elle a trouvé moyen d'irriter les deux puissances contre sa propre incapacité. L'abolition des corvées est devenue par sa faute une source de ruine pour les propriétaires, et une source de haine pour les paysans. Refusant d'accepter dans la constitution des points qui pouvaient assurer un développement des libertés communes à tous, et par là même *poloniser* le peuple, ils n'ont voulu en prendre que les moyens de turbulence, et conserver, dans une société basée sur l'égalité législative, leur ancienne position de caste. Qu'en devait-il résulter? Que l'Autriche s'est trouvée forte de toutes les sympathies du peuple, et l'idée d'une Pologne doublement haïe des paysans, tant par des souvenirs d'oppression que par le spectacle d'une émeute incessante contre les autorités protectrices! Par ainsi, notre noblesse a été la plus cruelle ennemie de ma patrie. Je n'ai pas caché mes opinions, je ne le devais pas. De là une haine de la part de ces gens qui n'ont rien appris et rien oublié – de là des calomnies obstinées – et en moi la conviction du *delenda est Carthago*. Ne comprenant même pas le communisme ils m'en accusent parce que ce mot effraie tout le monde, lorsque moi, je leur disais: avant tout, rendez au peuple le sentiment de sa nationalité en vous rapprochant de lui, et s'il le fallait aux dépens de quelques profits matériels! Le fol engouement pour Francfort *[sic]* et Kossuth m'a confirmé dans l'idée que notre noblesse ne saura jamais que perdre la patrie! Nos affaires, si belles en mars, sont presque désespérées aujourd'hui! La noblesse peut dans d'autres pays sauver la société – chez nous où elle a conservé des idées époque finie, il faut qu'elle finisse. Ne croyez pas leurs belles phrases! mensonge! J'y ai cru jadis et j'ai été amèrement détrompé. N'y-a-t-il donc aucun espoir? Il y en a un bien grand, mais sa réalisation dépend d'une fusion *politique* par de bonnes institutions communales, avant d'avoir été broyées par la révolution *sociale,* que ne repousse pas l'Autriche.[96]

Disappointment, frustration, and disillusionment with his fellow countrymen: these were Rzewuski's feelings as the year of revolution drew to a close. Certainly the failure of the revolutionary movement throughout Europe in 1848 and 1849 led its leaders and its thinkers to similar conclusions. For many the overthrow of the bright hopes they had entertained earlier, however bitter the situation now appeared, meant only a transference from one field of action to another. A large number of the men of '48 went into exile to await better times. In exile the refugees published their newspapers and pamphlets, pursued the arguments and factional quarrels begun before their flight abroad, and tried as best they could to keep in touch with their sympathizers at home, who were now deprived of all means of open expression. Such, however, was not to be Rzewuski's path. As Kieniewicz writes: 'He outdistanced his environment by the clarity of his judgement; he surpassed it in the courage of his opinions and the honesty of his intentions. But he lacked the determination to fight to the end.'[97] Already in 1849, while still continuing to write with sympathy about the ideas of agrarian socialism, he had begun to draw close to the circle gathered around his cousin, Adam Potocki, which was to provide the nucleus for a new Conservative party of the Galician Poles. 'The future,' he had written in 1848, 'does not belong to any party.'[98] But the political programme of Potocki's group and its organ *Czas (Time),* founded in Cracow in November 1848, was nevertheless in many ways congenial to Rzewuski's own way of thinking.

Decentralization of the Habsburg dominions, the development of communal self-government at the bottom, opposition both to the military-bureaucratic reaction and to doctrinaire liberalism, and the hand of friendship to the other Slav peoples in the Empire were all points in the group's platform which attracted Rzewuski. Although the Galician Conservative party was eventually to become the stronghold of the kind of reactionary obscurantism that Rzewuski had been battling with in '48 on the pages of *Progress,* at the beginning Potocki and his friends were still comparatively liberal in outlook and not yet bound firmly to the interests of the landed class.

This, and not any conscious betrayal of principles, helps to explain the transition from Rzewuski's populist socialism of 1848 to his close association with the Cracow Conservatives from 1849 onwards. To contemporaries and to later generations Rzewuski has been something of an enigma; for himself there was no inconsistency between the two positions.[99] We can detect here a close parallel between Rzewuski's socialism and that of the Christian socialists within the Church of England in the late 1840s and in the 1850s. (I have found no evidence, however, that they were aware of each other's existence, though many of their ideas had a common source in the doctrines of Buchez and Louis Blanc.) Rzewuski was of course writing in rural Galicia, and the needs of the village commune occupy the central place in his thinking; the English Christian socialists, on the other hand, had to fit their schemes into the framework of a highly industrialized economy. But they share in common an indifference to political forms and a reliance on apolitical economic co-operation, a disbelief in the desirability of an immediate application of full democracy, a strong distaste for the idea of class war or violent revolution, a longing to achieve a reconciliation on a lasting basis of the conflicting classes within the community, and finally the conviction that the landowning gentry, once it had shed its reactionary viewpoint, might still provide the leadership in the struggle for a new social order.

In contrast to Ściegienny or Dembowski, Rzewuski's populism was reformist. Sharply critical of his own class, he still sought its redemption, still hoped to see it lead in the struggle to achieve social change. However, in the situation in which the Poles found themselves after the successive disappointments of 1848 and 1863, legal populism, like revolutionary populism, had no prospect of success.

Epilogue

The failure of the new insurrection against the Russians, which broke out in January 1863, brought a fresh wave of exiles to join those already in the West. But neither in numbers nor in influence was the new emigration to equal its predecessor, the 'Great Emigration.' Agrarian socialist ideas, it is true, still found a number of adherents, while the revolutionary populist traditions of the communes of the 'Polish People' also remained alive; and Proudhon was particularly influential now, as were the Russians, Herzen, who had worked closely with Worcell in the 1850s, Bakunin, and Chernishevsky. At the same time the ideas of Marx and of Lassalle were spreading; within a dozen years the modern working-class movement, based on the industrial proletariat, made its first appearance on the Polish political scene.[1]

The Polish narodniks of the Great Emigration, in addition to deriving inspiration from Rousseau and the Jacobins, had drawn for their ideas upon every contemporary school of socialist thought. *Babouvisme* and Saint-Simonism; the Christian socialism of Buchez and the Christian democracy of Lamennais; Fourierism, Owenism, and the communism of Cabet; the anarchist mutualism of Proudhon; and the democratic socialism of Louis Blanc: all had their disciples among the Poles.[2] But Polish socialism of this period is not purely derivative. True, it produced no outstanding theorist, no major work; it made little impact outside the ranks of its own nationals, while in Poland itself, owing to political conditions, its influence was sporadic and impermanent. Nonetheless, in several respects its contribution was an original one. This originality stemmed from the differing circumstances in which Poland found herself when compared with Western Europe, from its agrarian economic structure and its loss of political independence.

Virtually without exception, of course, the émigré socialists were 'peasant' socialists. Like the later Russian populists, from Herzen down to the socialist revolutionaries, they wished to base socialism on the village and its institutions; they wished – and they believed it was in their power – to preserve their country from the evils of capitalism and the domination of the bourgeoisie by avoiding the kind of industrial development then taking place in the West. Secondly, they were all in varying degrees involved in the struggle to regain national independence. Their agrarian socialism, therefore, was strongly imbued with nationalism, however much the ultimate ideal of a world society might figure in their programmes. And it was the fact of foreign domination, combined with the backward social structure of the country and the lack of parliamentary government, that made a double revolution, to overthrow both the foreign and the domestic oppressor, seem essential. It was this that drove most of the Polish émigré narodniks, in contrast to the apolitical gradualism of the other Utopians in the West, to advocate, not peaceful means, but violence in order to bring in the new socialist order. Often disguising their thought in religious and mystical language the more radical, following in the *babouviste* tradition, put forward a doctrine of class-struggle – not, however, of proletarian against capitalist but of serf peasant against his lord. National independence, the social revolution, and the village commune: these three ideas were fundamental to their thinking.

The examples of Dembowski and Ściegienny, as well as of Stefański, the Woykowski circle, and Rzewuski (the last two reformists rather than revolutionaries), have shown that agrarian socialist ideas found acceptance in the 1840s among at least a few of those active in Poland in the independence movement. But the failure throughout Europe of the progressive cause in 1848-9 dealt the nationalist movement in Poland a blow from which it took more than a decade to recover.

The narodniks at home had drawn the inspiration for their hopes of a juster social order from the writings of the French Utopians, either direct or at second hand through their exiled fellow countrymen. But this had not entailed swallowing these doctrines whole, for the environment in which the Poles had to live and work differed greatly from that of their contemporaries in France and western Europe. Not only was Poland, in contrast to the West, an almost exclusively agricultural country, but it had also been deprived of its national independence. The attempt to regain their freedom therefore coloured the Poles' political activities at this period. And here the narodniks working in the home country were faced with a peculiar dilemma, which was posed for them much more acutely than for the émigrés, who could spin their dreams unrestrained by contact with harsh reality. The narodniks at home, on the other hand, found their populist ideals continuously at odds with their aims as nationalists. A socialist order was impossible so long as the partitioning powers remained in control of the country. It seemed equally clear that independence could be regained only through the united efforts of the gentry, who would provide the leadership, and of the peasantry, who would constitute a mass base for an army of liberation. But neither gentry nor peasantry would be won over to the national cause, at least in the foreseeable future, by any talk of socialist measures. Thus we see revolutionary populists like Dembowski for tactical reasons, somewhat akin perhaps to those of Lenin in 1917, temporarily putting aside their socialist principles and attempting to convert the peasantry to the national revolution by promising them full property rights in their holdings. 'These conspiratorial socialists, though with disgust, had finally to acquiesce in a simple granting of property.'[3] Without national independence the achievement of socialism was impossible. But in order to win independence the narodniks in Poland were constantly driven to abandon, at least for the time being, the propagation of their socialist ideals.

The exile narodniks had been the first in Eastern Europe to adapt and expand the ideas of the French Utopians to meet the needs of a country with an overwhelmingly agrarian economy. Their country, moreover, was engaged in a prolonged effort to regain its lost political independence: their adoption of populism and social revolution, they hoped, would help them achieve this goal. In the theories which emerged as a result of this intellectual encounter we meet from the beginning with much that is familiar later in the doctrines of Russian *narodnichestvo*: the class struggle of peasant with landowning gentry, the repartitional commune as the basis of a new socialist order through which the evils of industrial capitalism might be avoided, the transformation of the state into a free association of peasant communities, and even revolutionary slavophilism. Jacobin theories of a violent seizure of power and of terrorism, propounded in particular by the Polish People, also appear during the development of Russian populism, though here the religious garb in which the Poles clothed their ideas was almost completely absent. *Narodnichestvo* became a movement of much greater magnitude and influence. For agrarian socialism, despite its interesting beginnings, never took root in the intellectual tradition of the Polish left

– perhaps in part because, unlike in Russia, there were no communal institutions among the Polish peasants and artisans, no *mir* or *artel'* on which populists could pin their hopes and their illusions. Though a few isolated individuals in exile or at home were to espouse some variant of populism, they were drawn almost exclusively from the upper classes. The Polish peasantry remained almost entirely untouched. In fact the gentry intellectuals of the Polish People never succeeded in spreading their doctrines much beyond the narrow circle of the 'Portsmouth' soldiers. Yet it is with their 'movement to the people' in the early 1830s that the history of revolutionary populism in Eastern Europe begins.

Notes

PROLOGUE

1 For Herzen's contacts with the Poles in the 1850s, see Genowefa Kurpisowa,
   Aleksander Hercen a emigracja polska w latach 1847-1870 (Gdańsk 1964),
   chap. 2.
2 B. Nikolaievsky, ' "Za vashu i nashu vol'nost!" (Stranitsi iz istorii russko-
   pol'skikh otnoshenii),' *Novii Zhurnal* (New York), 7 (1944), pp. 261-9, has
   suggested that Herzen, as a result of his contacts (mainly through Bakunin)
   with Polish émigrés soon after his arrival in Paris early in 1847, may have derived part of the inspiration for his newly emerging populism (with its idealization of the peasant commune as the foundation on which to build the socialist Russia of the future) from the historical theories of the Polish historian
   Joachim Lelewel concerning the primitive Slav commune, which were extremely popular at that date among the Polish émigrés (see chap. 1, n. 5).
   Thus, writes Nikolaievsky, Lelewel may rightly be regarded as 'the ancestor
   not only of Polish, but also of Russian *narodnichestvo*.' I agree with Nikolaievsky that it is not at all impossible, too, that Herzen may have heard at
   the same time from his Polish connections of the ideas of the 'Polish People,'
   the émigré group chiefly responsible for propagating revolutionary populism
   among the Poles, and that he may have drawn on them at this period in
   shaping his political and social credo. See also Martin E. Malia, *Alexander
   Herzen and the Birth of Russian Socialism, 1812-1855* (Cambridge, Mass.
   1961), pp. 363, 366, 367, 393 ff., 473. Malia considers Nikolaievsky's hypothe-
   sis concerning the derivation of Herzen's theories on the peasant commune
   from Lelewel as 'intrinsically plausible,' though lacking 'direct evidence to
   support it' in Herzen's own writings. While ready to concede the influence of
   Polish left-wing ideas on Bakunin, the second great figure in the early history

of *narodnichestvo*, Malia does not refer specifically to a possible influence of the Polish People and its leaders on the Russian populists. Jan Kucharzewski, in his *Od białego caratu do czerwonego*, 2 (Warsaw 1925), pt 2, chap. 1, was perhaps the first to hint at this. For the impact of Lelewel's communalism on Bakunin in 1844, see Adam Leśniewski, *Bakunin a sprawy polskie w okresie Wiosny Ludów i powstania styczniowego 1863 roku* (Łódź 1962), pp. 17-19.

3 See my study 'Polish Nationalism,' pp. 310-72 in Peter F. Sugar and Ivo J. Lederer, eds, *Nationalism in Eastern Europe* (Seattle and London 1969; paperback edn 1971). In my article 'Z.D. Chodakowski and the discovery of folklife: a chapter in the history of Polish nationalism,' *Polish Review* (New York), 21 (1976), nos. 1-2, pp. 3-21, I have dealt with 'the intellectual ancestor of Polish populist nationalism,' who died in 1825.

4 Nineteenth-century Polish and Russian populism was both socialist and agrarian in character. But the term 'populism' has been applied to a wide – and confusing – variety of political doctrines and movements; its use has not been confined to those that have been agrarian or peasantist. See Ghiţa Ionescu and Ernest Gellner, eds, *Populism: Its Meanings and National Characteristics* (London 1969). In the present book, however, I have restricted its use to agrarian socialism in either a revolutionary or non-revolutionary form.

CHAPTER 1   THE BIRTH OF REVOLUTIONARY POPULISM

1 For general accounts, see Kalembka, *Wielka emigracja*, and – much less thorough – Günter Weber, *Die polnischen Emigration in neunzehnten Jahrhundert* (Essen 1937).

2 For Czartoryski as a political exile, see Marian Kukiel, *Czartoryski and European Unity 1770-1861* (Princeton 1955), chaps. 15-20. For Lelewel as an émigré politician, see Cygler, *Działalność polityczno-społeczna Joachima Lelewela*. For the Polish Democratic Society, see the long bibliographical note appended to my article 'The political program of the Polish Democratic Society,' *Polish Review* (New York), 14, no. 2 (Spring 1969), pp. 89-105, and no. 3 (Summer 1969), pp. 5-24. This study has been reprinted in my book, *Nationalism and Populism in Partitioned Poland*, pp. 59-101.

3 Quoted in Anna Rynkowska, 'Wojciech Darasz 1808-1852,' in Gąsiorowska, ed., *W stulecie Wiosny Ludów*, 4 (Warsaw 1951), p. 265.

4 The standard edition of Lelewel's writings on Poland was published in twenty volumes under the title *Polska, dzieje i rzeczy jej* (Poznań 1853-64). A new edition, which will include his complete works (*Dzieła*), is now in progress (Wrocław 1957 ff).

5 The historical theories of Lelewel, which he elaborated during his years of exile, also provided the main inspiration for a school of thought among the Poles that arose around the middle of the century. It may perhaps be considered as the counterpart in an agrarian society of the 'conservative' socialism existing in Germany about this time. The ideas of this group, whose members were to be found both in exile and in the home country, bear a resemblance on the one hand to those of the reactionary slavophils in contemporary Russia who wished to preserve the communal institutions of the Russian village as a bulwark against revolution and on the other (*mutatis mutandis*) to the land nationalization proposals of the Decembrist Pestel'. Poles of this school wished to make use of socialistic measures for the preservation of the existing order which, in their view, was otherwise threatened with collapse. Their main proposal was the introduction of collective ownership among the peasantry based upon the village commune, with the retention at the same time of private proprietorship for the estates of the gentry. Their advocacy of a limited socialism was conceived, therefore, as a protection against violent change. The former landlords were to receive compensation for giving up their rights over the peasants' holdings, and either the state or the individual communes, which were to administer the peasants' lands as a common concern of the whole village, would be responsible for its payment. This, together with the fact that the lord of the manor was usually assigned a deciding voice in the administration of the commune, gave such schemes, despite their socialistic colouring, a decided advantage in the eyes of most landowners over the proposals of the democrats, since the latter, while retaining private ownership in land, excluded the gentry from village life and deprived them of compensation. Most of the prominent representatives of this 'socialist' school, such as the philosopher F.B. Trentowski, belonged to the extreme conservative camp; though there were several liberals, such as the historian Jędrzej Moraczewski and the political theorist Karol Libelt, who held very similar views. See Mogilska, *Wspólna własność ziemi*, pp. 58-67, 69, 70.

6 For Polish exiles in England, see M.J.E. Copson-Niećko, 'Pro-Polish agitation in Great Britain 1832-1867,' PH D dissertation (University of London 1968); also Ludwik Zieliński, *Emigracja polska w Anglii w latach 1831-1846* (Gdańsk 1964). I have dealt with the Polish émigré left in England in a number of articles. Seven of these have been translated into Polish and published as a book, *Z dziejów Wielkiej Emigracji w Anglii* (Warsaw 1958). See also Henry G. Weisser, 'Polonophilism and the British working class 1830-1845,' *Polish Review* (New York), 12, no. 2 (Spring 1967), pp. 78-96, and his book *British Working-Class Movements and Europe 1815-48* (Manchester 1975), pp. 118-25.

7 See Stefania Sokołowska, *Młoda Polska: Z dziejów ugrupowań demokratycznych Wielkiej Emigracji* (Wrocław 1972). The organization was formed in Switzerland in the spring of 1834. It adopted a radical social programme, including the compulsory emancipation of the peasants and their endowment with the land they cultivated for their own use. This point was repeated in the programmes of Young Poland's successor organizations, the Confederation of the Polish People (1836-7) and the Union of the Polish Emigration (1837-46).

8 Bartkowski, *Wspomnienia*, p. 261.

9 *Krótki rys wypadków zaszłych w Ogóle Emigracji Polskiej w Londynie: Ogół Emigracji Polskiej w Londynie do całej emigracji polskiej* (Paris 1834), pp. 12-18; printed in my book *Geneza Ludu Polskiego w Anglii*, pt 4, no. 1. This book prints a large number of documents, mostly from manuscript, concerning the genesis of Polish revolutionary populism. It is cited below as GLP.

10 Worcell is the subject of a detailed and well written biography by Bolesław Limanowski, first published in Cracow in 1910 and several times reprinted. It still remains the major source of information for Worcell's activities and ideas.

11 See Tyrowicz, 'Drogi postępu radykalizmu społecznego Aleksandra Puławskiego,' *Kwartalnik Historyczny* (Warsaw), 63 (1956), no. 4/5, pp. 127-41; reprinted in his book *Z dziejów polskich ruchów społecznych*, pp. 35-61.

12 See my article 'Zeno Świętosławski, a forerunner of the Russian *narodniki*,' *American Slavic and East European Review* (New York), 13 (1954), no. 4, pp. 566-87, published in Polish translation in *Z dziejów Wielkiej Emigracji w Anglii*, pp. 64-94.

13 See Wajsblum, 'Od Belwederu do Leominster.'

14 See Bartkowski, *Wspomnienia*, passim.

15 See Łukaszewicz, *Tadeusz Krępowiecki*.

16 *Discours de Thadée Krempowiecki, prononcé à Paris le 29 novembre 1832, anniversaire de la révolution polonaise* (Paris 1833). See also Łukaszewicz, *Tadeusz Krępowiecki*, pp. 59-70. An annotated Polish translation of the speech is given by Łukaszewicz on pp. 148-62. Polish historians since the war have made much (perhaps a little too much) of Krępowiecki's utterances on this occasion. A good example of this is to be seen in the official university textbook which is being prepared by the Polish Academy of Sciences, *Historia Polski*, 3, pt 3 (Warsaw 1959), p. 76. Speaking of 'the tremendous significance' which the speech had 'for the further evolution of the Polish Democratic Society,' it goes on to describe it as 'a harbinger of a new phase in the development of the Polish revolutionary movement, the revolutionary democratic phase.'

17 Łukaszewicz, *Tadeusz Krępowiecki*, pp. 64-70

18 The 'Little Manifesto,' as the document is usually called, is reprinted in
Baczko, *Towarzystwo Demokratyczne Polskie*, pp. 3-8. Among its twenty-two
signatories were Krępowiecki, Puławski, and Świętosławski.

19 *Projekt do ustawy organicznej dla emigracji polskiej 1837 roku* (Paris 1837),
p. 5. This pamphlet prints the statutes of 1834 alongside those of 1837.

20 Cf. letter from F.K.H. Mackenzie of the Literary Association to Lord Dudley
Stuart, 9 June 1834, Harrowby Manuscripts (Sandon Hall), 26, pp. 166-7:
'The chief and really important matter for consideration is the surveillance to
be exercised over the moral and political conduct of the Polish emigrants ...
There is no question, My Lord, but that too many of the Poles now here are
ready to act upon the very worst radical principles. It requires little enquiry
to be satisfied of this – as also of the fact of their being strictly connected with
the Society of Amis des Droits at Paris. That Society is in constant and close
communication with, and even remits money to the leaders of our Unions,
who have emissaries over all France and in some parts of Germany. The in-
ference, as regards the Poles, is plain, and one condition should be, that the
Poles receiving aid shall [not] belong to *any* Union. It is also most important
that any breach of good morals should be subjected to punishment ... Sus-
pension and total removal from the list of pensioners should therefore be imposed as a punishment upon any group violation of morals being fully proved.
These are matters, My Lord, for your private consideration, not to be made
publicly known as odium would fall generally on the Poles; but to put you on
your guard and secure you from being reproached with having interested
yourself for unworthy objects.'

21 GLP, pt 4, no. 2, letter from Seweryn Dziewicki to Jan Bartkowski, 3 Sept.
1834, sewn into the fourth manuscript volume of Bartkowski's Memoirs (Bibliothèque Polonaise, Paris, ms. 422); it is also printed in Bartkowski,
Wspomnienia, pp. 446-9.

22 The main sources for developments among the Polish émigrés in London during the spring and summer of 1834 are to be found in the pamphlet already
cited, *Krótki rys*, and in Bartkowski's Memoirs, *Wspomnienia*. Both sources
are hostile to the leftists. See also Limanowski *Stanisław Worcell*, chap. 11;
Szpotański, 'Emigracja polska w Anglii,' pp. 284-87. Hitherto not much has
been known of the ideology of the left wing, which formed the London Commune. The pamphlet mentioned above, though including several of its documents, sheds little light on the Commune's political and social credo, while
Szpotański quotes only a revealing sentence or two from Dziewicki's interesting letter to Bartkowski referred to above. The archives of the Commune
have presumably perished, but those of the General Assembly of the London
Poles are still preserved in the Polish Library in Paris in twenty-three vol-

umes (mss. 587-608, formerly 419-423). They contain a number of documents of interest for the history of the Polish émigrés in Britain; they also provide almost the only source for the political and social doctrines of the London Commune of 1834. For this purpose three documents, copies made for their own use by the Commune's rivals, who controlled the exiles' General Assembly, are particularly valuable: the Statutes of the London Commune, issued on 6 Sept. (printed in GLP, pt 4, no. 3); its foundation manifesto of the same date, containing over ten large pages written in a minute hand (ibid., no. 4); and a declaration addressed by the Commune to the General Assembly of London Poles dated 17 Sept. (ibid., no. 6). My account is based largely on these documents.

23 'Gmina Londyńska Emigrantów Polskich do Emigracji Polskiej,' 6 Sept. 1834, GLP, pt 4, no. 4. The same ideas are also developed, though in less detail, in 'Gmina Emigracji Polskiej w Londynie do Ogółu Emigracji Polskiej,' 17 Sept. 1834, ibid., pt 5, no. 6.

24 The Statutes of the London Commune bring out clearly the tight discipline which was to be imposed on its members. Article 1 lays down that membership, once accepted, cannot be given up so long as the émigré is resident in London. Later articles provide for punishment and expulsion in the case of a betrayal of the Commune's principles. (This ban on voluntary resignation is reminiscent of the rules of the later Russian *Narodnaia Volia*, where there was a similar prohibition.) Article 3 begins as follows: 'Every member of the Commune bestows all his individual rights on the whole Commune.' Of course, as events were to prove, conditions prevailing in London in the 1830s deprived the 'Jacobins' of the Polish Commune of any real authority over their fellow members.

25 See J.L. Talmon, *The Origins of Totalitarian Democracy* (London 1952).

26 Dziewicki's letter to Bartkowski, cited above in n. 21.

27 See my article 'The birth of Polish socialism' (also published in translation in my *Z dziejów Wielkiej Emigracji*, pp. 39-63).

28 Cf. Mikos, 'W sprawie składu społecznego ... Ludu Polskiego.' For lack of evidence the precise social status of many of the Portsmouth soldiers remains so far an open question. However, a considerable number of them clearly came from a peasant background. Even in cases where men had done many years' service in the regular Polish army before the uprising, I cannot agree with Mikos that they were not likely to have retained 'the mentality of serf peasants' (p. 673). The pronouncements put out in their name in later years, though not definitive evidence, would seem to indicate the reverse; and the general opinion in the emigration appears to bear this out (see, for example, the letter from Lach Szyrma to Adam Czartoryski, 29 Jan. 1834, Czartoryski Library, Cracow, ms. 5521, p. 20).

29 See Ludwik Zieliński, 'Przyczynek do dziejów Gromady Grudziąż Ludu Polskiego,' *Gdańskie Zeszyty Humanistyczne* (Gdańsk), no. 1-2 (1960), pp. 81-109, for new material on the arrival of the soldiers in the West taken from former Prussian archives now in Gdańsk.

30 Letter from Szyrma to Czartoryski's secretary, Hipolit Błotnicki, 5 Sept. 1834, Czartoryski Library, ms. 5522, p. 579

31 Letter from Szyrma to Błotnicki, 2 Sept. 1834, ibid., p. 560. Cf. W.A. Smith, delegate of the conservatively inclined Literary Association of the Friends of Poland, to its honorary secretary K.J.H. Mackenzie, 17 Sept. 1834: 'We have had the *damn'dest* row today with the soldiers, the Priest, Stawiarski ... Stawiarski is bad enough – is too bad – but the Priest is ten times worse' (ibid., p. 603).

32 *Okólniki Towarzystwa Demokratycznego Polskiego* (Poitiers 1835), no. 791, p. 191, in GLP, pt 5, no. 16

33 Stawiarski to Worcell, 19 Sept. 1834, 'Szczątki wojska polskiego w Anglii' (Bibliothèque Polonaise, ms. 587 [vol. II]).

34 See my article 'The birth of Polish socialism,' p. 218.

35 Stawiarski to Lord Dudley Stuart (rough draft), 6 April 1835, Bibliothèque Polonaise, ms. 607 (vol. XXII). Cf. the letter from Stawiarski to General Dwernicki, 9 April 1835: 'Until Dziewicki's arrival ... we lived among ourselves like brothers, we all shared the same political principles aiming at a free, equal, undivided and independent Poland. Dziewicki, under cover of so-called ultra-democracy, having deluded many of the less educated brethren with various promises of money from Galicia, Poznania and the French people ... has secretly formed a gang with whom he frequents the taverns, drinking hard himself and encouraging the others to get drunk. He preaches to them that all officers are their enemies, that they must wipe them out along with the gentry, that anyone who is not for them should be killed off.' For Dudley Stuart, see M. Kukiel's article in *Wiadomości* (London), 16 Jan. 1955, no. 459.

36 A useful source for establishing the chronology of events in Portsmouth is Stawiarski's diary, 'Dziennik emigracji polskiej w Portsmouth,' Bibliothèque Polonaise, ms. 587 (vol. I).

37 *Okólniki Towarzystwa Demokratycznego Polskiego* (1835), no. 457, pp. 119-25. According to the list of members dated 20 March 1835, there were 23 members in the Jersey section out of a total of 1193 in the whole Society. Whereas the later issues of the Society's 'circulars' (*okólniki*), a kind of information bulletin for the private use of its members, are printed, those for 1834-7 are still merely lithographed. The bound volume of the early series in the Polish Library in Paris is, I believe, the only one now in existence.

38 Papers of Colonel Józef Święcicki, Muzeum Adama Mickiewicza, Paris, ms. 1062, 12 May 1835, GLP, pt 5, no. 13

39 *Okólniki T.D.P.* (1835), no. 791, pp. 181, 182, in GLP, pt 5, no. 9
40 6 May 1835, ibid., no. 671, p. 154, in GLP, pt 5, no. 12
41 25 May 1835, ibid., no. 791, pp. 186, 187, in GLP, pt 5, no. 15
42 15 July 1835, ibid., p. 191, in GLP, pt 5, no. 15. The Central Section was right in its assessment of the feeling throughout the Society. As it turned out, almost all the sections condemned social violence and wholeheartedly supported the official line of emancipating the peasantry with full property rights to the land they tilled. They saw in this policy the only hope of winning over both gentry and peasantry in the home country to support a forthcoming uprising. See ibid., 1835: no. 1090, pp. 215-40; 1836: no. 172, pp. 21-24, no. 338, pp. 46, 47, no. 540, p. 64. For the views of the socialistically inclined dissidents within the Society's ranks, see Baczko, *Towarzystwo Demokratyczne Polskie,* pp. 53-70, 97-108.
43 Father Pułaski, who also left Jersey at this time, did not, however, become a member of the Polish People. The reasons for this are not at all clear. From this date until his death in 1838 he seems to have withdrawn from active participation in émigré politics.
44 Baczko, *T.D.P.,* pp. 353-7
45 The document defines the 'people' as follows: 'It is not merely a certain section of the community, it is not merely a certain number of the inhabitants who possess such and such amount of land, such and such property. But the expression – the people – in the sense in which we use it, embraces all persons without exception and therefore the interest of the people is that of all members of the community' (ibid., p. 354). Like Blanqui's proletariat of 'thirty million Frenchmen,' the term was not yet clearly defined in the sense of a social class; it had not yet advanced much beyond the eighteenth-century concept.
46 Temkinowa, *Lud Polski,* pp. 53-64

CHAPTER 2 POLISH NARODNIKS IN EXILE

1 For recent studies of its history and ideology, see Mikos, *Gromady Ludu Polskiego w Anglii*; Temkinowa, *Gromady Ludu Polskiego*; Krysanka, 'Z dziejów Gromady Grudziąż Ludu Polskiego'; and Ciołkosz, *Zarys dziejów socjalizmu polskiego,* 1, pp. 104-47. See also Marian Tyrowicz, 'Kilka kwestii z rozwoju organizacyjnego Ludu Polskiego (1837-1846) w świetle najnowszej historiografii, '*Przegląd Historyczny* (Warsaw), 56 (1965), no. 4, pp. 651-7. Almost the only primary source for its history is to be found in the documents published by Zeno Świętosławski in Jersey in 1854: *Lud Polski w emigracji, 1835-1846.* The more important of these have been reprinted in Temkinowa, *Lud Polski.*

2 Temkinowa, *Lud Polski*, p. 227. (They may also have known something of Pestel's scheme for partial nationalization of the land.) See Worcell's speech in Jersey at a memorial meeting for Buonarroti who died in 1837 (ibid., pp. 217-27). In it he says: 'Buonarroti was the first writer to proclaim the principle of *l'égalité des conditions sociales*. The Grudziąż Commune publicly accepted this principle as its own on behalf of the Polish people ... After France he [Buonarroti] loved Poland with a special affection, regarding her as a sister in devotion beside his beloved France ... Among the émigrés there was a chosen handful whom he loved above the rest ... This was the handful of the lowly of this world made up of poor peasants (whom Christ also loved and cared for), the Portsmouth soldiers, the only representatives of the oppressed masses of Poland, in other words, the Grudziąż Commune. Why should I not place in front of your eyes proofs of that fatherly concern with which he encompassed them?'

3 Ibid., pp. 350, 375

4 Gryzelda Missalowa, 'Francuski socjalizm utopijny i jego wpływ na polską myśl rewolucyjną w latach 1830-1848,' in Gąsiorowska, ed., *W stulecie Wiosny Ludów*, III, pt 2, p. 115. The first Pole to be converted to socialism was probably Bohdan Jański, who joined the Saint-Simonians as a student in Paris before the 1830 insurrection. By 1832 he had drifted away from their movement.

5 Temkinowa, *Lud Polski,* pp. 55, 57, 71, 116-17, 123, 195. Polemics with the Democratic Society, which began even before the founding of the Polish People, are found scattered throughout its pronouncements.

6 Ibid., pp. 54, 58, 61, 69, 93, 96

7 Ibid., pp. 93, 96. The Polish People held that the Christian church had advocated communism until it was corrupted by the ruling caste and its tools, the priests. Primitive Christianity had been revived by Robespierre and his cult of the Supreme Being. Paris had then become 'the capital of a new papacy,' Rome the seat of Antichrist (see ibid. pp. 92, 112, 206-7.) The influence of Lamennais's anti-clerical version of Christianity is apparent here as in the writings of many other Polish left-wing 'Catholics' of this period.

8 Ibid., pp. 60, 63, 69, 89

9 Ibid., pp. 79, 82, 84, 125, 127, 202. The contrast between the decadent, capitalist West and the 'young' Slav world preserving intact elements of a primitive socialism is to be found in the thought of the Polish People and some of the other Polish agrarian socialists. But it is much less pronounced than, for instance, with Herzen and the Russian narodniks – because of the strength of anti-Russian feeling among the Poles.

10 Ibid., pp. 82-4

11 Ibid., pp. 168-70

12 Ibid., pp. 82, 125, 202-5
13 'The property of today was born simply of plunder' (Własność dzisiejsza urodziła się po prostu z grabieży), ibid., p. 201. This statement, which was probably Worcell's, occurs several years before Proudhon's famous maxim appeared in print. The idea in almost identical phrasing also occurs in France at the end of the eighteenth century.
14 Reprinted ibid., pp. 135-59. The essay was completed in 1836.
15 Duker, 'Polish *Émigré* Christian Socialists on the Jewish problem,' pp. 322-3. Duker detects an anti-semitic element in Worcell's writings. He does in fact attack Jewish finance capital in his essay on property. Describing the effects of the rapid spread of capitalism in Poland, which he alleges would result from carrying out the Democratic Society's policy, he exclaims: 'Fertile Poland suddenly condemned to eternal hunger! Christian Poland suddenly given over into the hands of the Jews to be beaten ... and crucified by them' (Temkinowa, *Lud Polski*, pp. 149-50). Such sentiments, however, do not necessarily have a racial connotation: similar passages may be found, for instance, in the editorials of the Chartist Ernest Jones's *People's Paper* or in the writings of some west European socialists of the period. Cf. also the same kind of 'anti-semitism' in the writings of the home country revolutionary populist, Father Piotr Ściegienny (see below, chap. 3). Even the poverty-stricken village Jew, Ściegienny wrote in his 'Little Golden Book,' lives by exploitation of the peasant and rural artisan – just like their numerous gentile exploiters from the monarch downwards ('Złota książeczka czyli historia rodu ludzkiego' [1840], in D'iakov, *Piotr Ściegienny*, p. 218).
16 This argument had been used earlier by the Portsmouth socialists to support collective ownership (see Temkinowa, *Lud Polski*, p. 411). It was also frequently employed by the Democratic Society in defence of private property.
17 For their contacts with the British left, see my article 'Polish Democrats and English Radicals, 1832-1862: a chapter in the history of Anglo-Polish relations,' *Journal of Modern History* (Chicago), 25 (1953) no. 2, pp. 142-4 (also published in Polish translation in my *Z dziejów Wielkiej Emigracji*, pp. 13-38).
18 Temkinowa, *Lud Polski*, pp. 20, 84, 127
19 Baczko, *T.D.P.*, pp. 98-108, 124-5; see also pp. 59-60.
20 Ibid., pp. 99-102
21 Ibid., pp. 107-8
22 Ibid., p. 103. In using this last phrase the writers show themselves nearer in spirit to the main body of opinion in the Society, which regarded the minor gentry as one of the mainstays of Polish democracy, than to the anti-gentry class consciousness of the Polish People.
23 Ibid., pp. 102-7

24 See Helena Łuczakówna, *Wiktor Heltman, 1796-1874* (Poznań 1935).
25 For the schism of 1837-8, which led to the explusion of Dziewicki and Krępowiecki from the Polish People, see my article, 'Na marginesie historii Gromady Grudziąż,' *Przegląd Historyczny*, 52 (1961), no. 1, pp. 87-111; no. 2, pp. 274-96. This includes the transcription of a lengthy document from the Bibliothèque Polonaise in Paris. (See also Irena Koberdowa, 'Rozłam w Gromadzie Grudziądż Ludu Polskiego w 1838 r. według dokumentów Ogółu,' pp. 187-92 in *Studia historyczne* (Warsaw 1965) – a Festschrift for Stanisław Arnold.) The two dissidents set up their own organization (Wyznawcy obowiązków społecznych) which, along with another socialist splinter group, the Le Havre Commune, formed the left wing of the centrist Union of the Polish Emigration until its dissolution in 1846. See Ciołkosz, *Zarys dziejów socjalizmu polskiego*, 1, pp. 148-64; Cygler, *Zjednoczenie Emigracji Polskiej 1837-1846* (Gdańsk 1963), pp. 153-60.
26 There are biographies of Konarski by Witold Łukaszewicz (1948) and Henryk Mościcki (1949), both published in Warsaw.
27 For Czyński's socialism, see Ciołkosz, *Zarys dziejów socjalizmu polskiego*, 1, pp. 199-222.
28 'Zbrodnie ludu są skutkiem źle urządzonego społeczeństwa,' quoted by Mościcki, *Szymon Konarski*, p. 34
29 The Statutes *Ustawy Kościoła Powszechnego* are reprinted in full in Temkinowa, *Lud Polski*, pp. 230-315. See D'iakov, *Piotr Ściegienny*, p. 162, for the many parallels between the Statutes and the politico-social programme of Świętosławski's contemporary, Father Ściegienny. The Statutes of course were finished only in the year of Ściegienny's arrest (see below, chap. 3).
30 See Turowski, *Utopia społeczna Ludwika Królikowskiego*; Ciołkosz, *Zarys dziejów socjalizmu polskiego*, 1, pp. 178-99. A selection from Królikowski's writings has recently been published: *Wybór pism*, ed. Adam Sikora and Hanna Temkinowa (Warsaw 1972).
31 *Système de fraternité* (Paris), no. 4 (1850), p. 114. Christopher H. Johnson in his *Utopian Communism in France: Cabet and the Icarians 1839-1851* (Ithaca and London 1974) notes that Królikowski's influence led Cabet to stress Christian ideas from 1842 on (see pp. 93, 259).
32 See especially 'O zjednoczeniu,' *Polska Chrystusowa* (Paris), 2 (1843), pp. 209-383; 'Ojczyzna matka do swoich dzieci,' *Zbratnienie* (Paris 1847), pp. 16-64.
33 In a letter to *Zbratnienie* (12 April 1847) Świętosławski takes Królikowski to task for his neglect of all forms of political organization above the level of the commune. Królikowski, on the other hand, criticized Świętosławski for attempting in his statutes to provide a too rigid political framework.
34 'Urządzenie gminy,' *Polska Chrystusowa*, 2, pp. 393-415

35 For Fourier's influence in Russia at this period, see F.I. Kaplan, 'Russian Fourierism of the 1840s: a contrast to Herzen's Westernism,' *American Slavic and East European Review* (New York), 17 (1958), no. 2, pp. 161-72.
36 Królikowski strongly objected to this proposal, which he considered would help prolong the existing social order, the rule of Satan ('Zbawienie tylko w Chrystusie,' *Polska Chrystusowa*, 2, pp. 415-33).
37 Weintraub, 'Adam Mickiewicz.' Much of what I have written in this section is based on this penetrating study, which is also most useful on account of its extensive bibliographical data. See also Drobner, *Mickiewicz jako socjalista.*
38 See Kieniewicz, *Legion Mickiewicza*, pp. 73-9. The Principles were translated into French as *Symbole politique de la Pologne renaissante.*
39 Adam Mickiewicz, *Dzieła*, ed. Julian Krzyżanowski et al., 12 (Warsaw 1955), pp. 7, 8, 323, 324. Cf. Weintraub, 'Adam Mickiewicz,' pp.167-9.
40 This is Weintraub's interpretation. He writes: 'The cake was to be preserved for the landlord and eaten by the peasants. The Manifesto reveals an embarrassing inability to think in terms of concrete social conditions' ('Adam Mickiewicz,' p. 169).
41 Mickiewicz's contributions have been reprinted in a French edition edited by his son Władysław, *La Tribune des peuples* (Paris 1907). (A phototype edition of the journal was published in Wrocław in 1963.) See also Łukaszewicz, 'Trybuna Ludów,' *Prace Polonistyczne*, (Wrocław), 11 (1953), especially pp. 255-74; Weintraub, 'Adam Mickiewicz,' pp. 169-73.
42 See *Polski słownik biograficzny* (Cracow), II (1936), pp. 408, 409. In addition to helping *La Tribune des peuples* Branicki gave financial support at this period for Proudhon's publications.
43 Among these the most important was the Proudhonist Karol Edmund Chojecki (pseudonym Charles Edmond). See *P.S.B.*, III (1937), pp. 391-2; Ciołkosz, *Zarys dziejów socjalizmu polskiego*, 1, pp. 337-47. The paper's collaborators also included several conservatives, followers of Prince Czartoryski.
44 'Notre Programme,' *La Tribune des peuples* (1907 edn), p. 58
45 'Le Socialisme,' ibid., pp. 162-75
46 Mickiewicz, *Dzieła*, 12, pp. 116-20
47 'De l'idée napoléonienne,' *La Tribune des peuples* (1907 edn), pp. 274-6
48 Mickiewicz's importance in the development of European radicalism is shown in his influence on Lamennais. See Manfred Kridl, 'Two champions of a New Christianity: Lamennais and Mickiewicz,' *Comparative Literature* (Eugene, Oregon), 4 (1952), no. 3, pp. 239-67.
49 Rzadkowska, *Działalność Centralizacji T.D.P.*, chap. 2, gives an account of the Society's sociopolitical ideology in the 1850s. See also Józef Żmigrodzki, 'Towarzystwo Demokratyczne Polskie w okresie schyłkowym (1847-1862),'

Rocznik Polskiego Towarzystwa Naukowego na Obczyźnie: Rok 1953-1954 (London), pp. 31-3.

50 See Podolecki, *Wybór pism*. Podolecki was a member of the Society's central committee *(Centralizacja)* in London between 1849 and 1851.

51 'Towarzystwo Demokratyczne Polskie i kwestie socjalne,' *Demokrata Polski* (1852), reprinted in Baczko, *T.D.P.*, pp. 324-36. See also Groniowski, *Problem rewolucji agrarnej*, p. 69.

52 'Znaczenie rewolucji socjalnej w Europie i w Polsce,' *Demokrata Polski* (1851), quoted in Podolecki, *Wybór pism,* p. 292. I have not been able to trace any contacts between the Polish Democratic Society and the contemporary English Christian socialists, also disciples of Buchez. Podolecki had been a member in the early 1840s of a short-lived organization, Polish Democracy of the Nineteenth Century, founded by Józef Ordęga with a programme based on Buchez's social and religious principles. See Kostołowski, *Studia nad kwestią włościańską* pp. 29 ff.

53 In addition to my article, 'The Polish revolutionary commune' (also published in Polish translation in my *Z dziejów Wielkiej Emigracji*, pp. 95-110), see also Knapowska, 'Lud Polski – Gromada Rewolucyjna Londyn'; Miller, 'Dokoła genezy Gromady Rewolucyjnej Londyn'; Romaniukowa, 'Dalsze dokumenty'; S.M. Fal'kovich, 'Levye techeniia v pol'skoi emigratsii nakanune vosstaniia 1863 g.,' in V.A. D'iakov et al., eds, *Russko-pol'skie revoliutsionnye sviazi 60-kh godov i vosstanie 1863 goda* (Moscow 1962), pp. 77-103, 144-46. For the doctrines of the Revolutionary Commune's Paris sympathizer, Dr. F.K. Zawadzki, see Ciołkosz, *Zarys dziejów socjalizmu polskiego*, 1, pp. 433-42. (The Ciolkoszes deal in general with émigré socialism of the 1850s on pp. 390-486 of their first volume.)

54 This point was brought out in the Revolutionary Commune's programme as well as in that of its predecessor, the Society of the Polish Emigration (Towarzystwo Emigracji Polskiej zasad gminowładno-społecznych). This society existed from 1853 until its fusion with the newly founded Revolutionary Commune in 1856. In an address dated 27 Feb. 1855 it stated: 'For the basis of the edifice, and the model of the future social reform, we adopt the Commune, as restoring the patriarchal life of the Slavonian, and suitable to the desires of the people.' From 'The Committee of the Society of the Polish Emigration, representing the Polish Democracy at the Commemoration of the Great Revolutionary Movement of 1848, to the whole Polish Democratic Emigration,' printed in the *People's Paper* (London), 17 March 1855; reprinted in my article 'Polish socialists in early Victorian England: three documents,' *Polish Review* (New York), 6, no. 1-2 (Winter-Spring 1961), p. 45.

1 *Communist Manifesto*, ed. Harold J. Laski (London 1948), p. 167. In Polish there are three monographs on the events of 1846 in Cracow and neighbouring Galicia: Stefan Kieniewicz, *Ruch chłopski w Galicji w 1846 roku* (Wrocław 1951); Czesław Wycech, *Powstanie chłopskie w roku 1846* (Warsaw 1955); and Marian Żychowski, *Rok 1846 w Rzeczypospolitej Krakowskiej i Galicji* (Warsaw 1956). In English we now have an account in Kieniewicz's synthesis, *The Emancipation of the Polish Peasantry*, chap. 9, and another in Thomas W. Simons jr, 'The Peasant Revolt of 1846 in Galicia: recent Polish historiography,' *Slavic Review* (Seattle), 30 (1971), no. 4, pp. 795-817. The latest addition to the literature is Arnon Gill, *Die polnische Revolution 1846: Zwischen nationalem Befreiungskampf des Landadels und antifeudaler Bauernerhebung* (Munich and Vienna 1974).

2 See R.F. Leslie, 'Left-wing political tactics in Poland, 1831-46,' *Slavonic and East European Review* (London), 33, no. 80 (December 1954), pp. 120-39, and his *Reform and Insurrection in Russian Poland 1856-1865* (London 1963), chap. 1. The literature in Polish is too large to list here; see the bibliography in Leslie's book.

3 There is an extensive literature on the conspiratorial movement in Poland during the decade and a half after the 1830 uprising. Most of the important works (to 1957) are listed in Witold Łukaszewicz, 'Ruch rewolucyjny w kraju 1830-1845, '*Prace Polonistyczne* (Łódź), 13 (1957), pp. 308-12. Lidia and Adam Ciołkosz, in their *Zarys dziejów socjalizmu polskiego*, 1, deal with Polish agrarian socialism in the homeland before 1848 on pp. 223-66.

4 Ściegienny died in 1890. For his ideas and activities, see especially Tyrowicz, *Sprawa ks. Piotra Ściegiennego*; Wycech, *Ks. Piotr Ściegienny*; D'iakov, *Piotr Ściegienny*. All three volumes reprint selections from Ściegienny's writings and contain extensive bibliographical data. D'iakov's survey of the literature to date (on pp. 19-25) is particularly valuable; in addition, his book presents a rich selection from the archival materials relating to Ściegienny, which he uncovered recently in Moscow. See also Młynarski, *W kręgu sprawy ks. Piotra Ściegiennego*, and Valenta, 'Petr Ściegienny.'

5 See above, chap. 1.

6 Probably composed about 1840-2, the Letter has been several times reprinted. It exists in more than one variant. The first reliable transcription of one of these was given by Balicka in 'Legenda.' D'iakov, *Piotr Ściegienny*, pp. 238-64, prints another variant. It is interesting to note that around the turn of the century the Letter was adapted more than once for use as socialist propaganda. Several writers (e.g. Młynarski, *W kręgu sprawy Ściegiennego*, chap. 6)

have cast doubt on Ściegienny's authorship; this seems, however, to be fairly well established. In any event the Letter certainly reflects his viewpoint accurately.

7 Agaton Giller, *Historja powstania narodu polskiego w 1861-1864 r.*, 3 (Paris 1870), pp. 512-15; and his *Karol Ruprecht: Szkic biograficzny* (Lvov 1875), pp. 42, 43; *Pamiętniki Szymona Tokarzewskiego*, 1: *Siedem lat katorgi* (Warsaw 1907), pp. 3-7; 2: *Ciernistym szlakiem* (Warsaw 1909), pp. 15, 16, 28. Both Giller and Tokarzewski tend to underestimate outside influences on Ściegienny's political thought.

8 'Aforyzmy czyli rzucone myśli do odszukania i oznaczenia źródła nieszczęść ród ludzki trapiących' (1857), quoted in Wycech, *Ks. Piotr Ściegienny*, p. 167. Ściegienny had developed this idea earlier in the Letter of Gregory XVI: e.g. 'God created men – and you too – in order that they should freely use all God's gifts'; 'God gave us the earth which nourishes us ... therefore, O man, if you allow it to be taken away from you ... [it is] not by God's will, but by your own;' 'God having created man placed him upon the earth which he ordained ... for all men and allowed him to use all the fruits of the earth obtained by labour. Nevertheless man paid nothing to God either for the land on which he dwelt or for the produce of the earth from which he gained nourishment.' In such phrases as these Ściegienny was probably echoing the reference in the Polish Democratic Society's Little Manifesto of 1832 to 'the earth and all its fruits common to all men' (wspólna dla wszystkich ziemia i jej owoce), which we have seen, had been mistakenly regarded by the Society's left wing as an affirmation of socialism. Ściegienny may also have been influenced by medieval Catholic political theory, which was in some ways similar to the viewpoint he propounds.

9 This was the amount of land traditionally considered sufficient to maintain the 'full-peasant,' the most well-to-do member of his class, together with his family. See Leslie, *Polish Politics and the Revolution of November 1830* (London 1956), pp. 56-61.

10 Giller, *Historia powstania*, 3, p. 513

11 Balicka, 'Ksiądz Piotr Ściegienny,' in *Księga pamiątkowa ku uczczeniu ... Marcelego Handelsmana* (Warsaw 1929), p. 80; Ściegienny, 'Aforyzmy o urządzeniu społeczeństwa ludzkiego,' pp. 265-95, in D'iakov, *Piotr Ściegienny*. See also Tokarzewski, *Pamiętniki*, 1, p. 16.

12 'Dążność, obowiązki i przeznaczenie chrześcijaństwa dla ludu wiejskiego i miejskiego napisane' (1876), in Wycech, *Ks. Piotr Ściegienny*, p. 192

13 Giller, *Historia powstania*, 3, p. 514

14 See Włodzimierz Dzwonkowski, 'Na marginesie monografii o ruchach rewolucyjnych w Królestwie Kongresowym w latach1835-1845,' *Myśl Współczesna*

(Warsaw-Łódź), no. 11-12 (1948), pp. 97-103, 106-10, 120-4. Social revolutionary ideas were brought by young emissaries of the émigré left wing to Austrian Galicia in the early 1830s and from there spread across the borders into the Russian-occupied Congress Kingdom.

15 Tokarzewski in his Memoirs (*Pamiętniki*, 2, p. 20) relates that among these emissaries was to be found the young son of Zeno Świętosławski, a leading figure in the émigré organization the Polish People (see above, chap. 1). This statement has been repeated by later writers anxious to establish a definite link between Ściegienny and the socialists in exile. But at this time Świętosławski's eldest son could have been no more than ten years old at the most!

16 Tokarzewski, *Pamiętniki*, 1, p. 5

17 See Franciszek Paprocki, 'Walenty Stefański jako działacz Związku Plebeuszy,' in Gąsiorowska, ed., *W stulecie Wiosny Ludów*, 4, pp. 351-94.

18 Andrzej Wojtkowski, 'Poglądy pisarzy poznańskich pierwszej połowy wieku XIX na epoki w historji,' *Kronika Miasta Poznania*, 3 (1925), no. 11, pp. 220-4

19 Quoted in *Pamiętniki ś.p. Aleksandra Guttrego z lat 1845, 46, 47*, 1, (Poznań 1891), p. 36. See also Franciszek Wiesiołowski, *Pamiętnik z r. 1845-1846* (Lvov 1868), p. 61.

20 Ibid., pp. 62-5. See also Zdzisław Grot and Franciszek Paprocki, *Szkice poznańskie 1794-1864* (Warsaw 1957), p. 84.

21 See below, pp. 59-65.

22 Contacts were maintained with the German socialist group in Breslau. An interesting indication of the strongly nationalist colouring of the Union of Plebeians was the ruling made by Stefański that no Protestants should be admitted to membership – 'Protestant' and 'German' being almost interchangeable in the Poznań area. Stefański's anti-Germanism, however, had a social rather than a national character. See Tyrowicz, *Udział Śląska w ruchu rewolucyjnym 1846-1849* (Warsaw 1949), pp. 46, 50, 53, 71 ff.; Paprocki in Gąsiorowska, *W stulecie Wiosny Ludów*, 4, pp. 364, 377, 378; Bohdan Zakrzewski, 'Z dziejów walki,' p. 291. Zakrzewski's study has also been published separately (Poznań 1953).

23 Władysław Kosiński, *Sprawa polska z roku 1846 przed sąd opinii publicznej wytoczona* (Poznań 1850), p. 56

24 Until recently it was thought that the opinions recorded by Kosiński, who does not mention anyone by name, were those of Stefański. But Zakrzewski, 'Z dziejów walki,' pp. 290, 344-9, has shown on the basis of an autograph note in Kosiński's own copy of his book that it is to Mikorski and not to Stefański that he is referring.

25 Kosiński, *Sprawa polska*, pp. 56-8. Kosiński optimistically believed (pp. 59-

63) even as late as 1850 that if an uprising were to break out the gentry might in fact be persuaded on grounds of Christian brotherhood to give over their property to be administered by a village council for the period of hostilities – on the understanding that a final decision would only be reached at the conclusion of the uprising.

26 For the political and social ideas of the Woykowski circle, see Zakrzewski, 'Z dziejów walki,' pp. 312-75. See also Zenon Kosidowski, *Z okresu złotego kultury Poznania: Tygodnik Literacki 1838-1845* (Poznań 1938); Maria Frelkiewicz, *Julia Molińska-Woykowska: Próba monografii* (Poznań 1938); Zakrzewski, *Tygodnik Literacki.*

27 *Tygodnik Literacki* (1843), no. 7, p. 41 (quoted by Zakrzewski, 'Z dziejów walki,' p. 328)

28 Ibid. (1844), no. 13, p. 100 (quoted by Zakrzewski, 'Z dziejów walki,' p. 343)

29 Tadeusz Gospodarek, *Julia Molińska-Woykowska (1816-1851)* (Wrocław 1962), p. 77

30 *Tygodnik Literacki* (1844), no. 18, p. 140 (quoted by Zakrzewski, 'Z dziejów walki,' p. 341)

31 The most detailed treatment of Dembowski's ideas is to be found in Narsky, *Mirovozzrenie E. Dembovskogo;* Śladkowska, *Poglądy;* Ładyka, *Dembowski,* which includes selected writings. Przemski, *Edward Dembowski,* is a readable study of his life and writings. See also Stecka, *Edward Dembowski; Polski słownik biograficzny,* 5 (Cracow 1939-46), pp. 85-7. There is a collected edition of his works, *Pisma,* ed. Anna Śladkowska and Maria Żmigrodzka, 5 vols (Warsaw 1955).

32 See Poniatowski, *O poglądach Kamieńskiego;* Witold Kula, 'Henryk Kamieński,' in Gąsiorowska, *W stulecie Wiosny Ludów,* IV, pp. 313-50.

33 See Tyrowicz, *Julian Maciej Goslar: Zarys życia i materiały biograficzne* (Warsaw 1953). A revised and expanded version of the biographical sections of Tyrowicz's study has since been published as *Prawda i mit biografii Goslara,* but this version omits the source materials appended to the earlier edition.

34 Tyrowicz, *Julian Maciej Goslar,* p. 124. The text of Goslar's appeal is given on pp. 123-34 of the 1953 edition.

35 Ibid., p. 129, where Goslar admits the possibility of hired labour for their cultivation.

36 This had probably been composed by Libelt at the direction of the Democratic Society already before the revolution. See Tyrowicz, *Jan Tyssowski, dyktator krakowski z r. 1846* (Warsaw 1930), p. 110.

37 Cited from Tyrowicz, ed., *Galicja od pierwszego rozbioru do Wiosny Ludów 1771-1849* (Cracow-Wrocław 1956), pp. 191-3. Cf. Bartel, 'Rewolucja

krakowska,' pp. 185-6. See also Henry G. Weisser, 'The British working class and the Cracow uprising of 1846,' *Polish Review* (New York), 13, no. 1 (Winter 1968), which gives a contemporary English translation of the Manifesto on pp. 18-19, and the same author's note, 'New light on the Cracow Manifesto,' ibid., 16, no. 2 (Spring 1971), pp. 103, 104, as well as his book *British Working-Class Movements and Europe 1815-48* (Manchester 1975), pp. 140-4.

38 Henryk Kamieński, *O prawdach żywotnych narodu polskiego* (Brussels 1844), reprinted in *Wybór pism*, pp. 206-18

39 Kamieński, *Filozofia ekonomii materialnej ludzkiego społeczeństwa*, 2 (Poznań 1844), in *Wybór pism*, p. 176

40 Kosiński, *Sprawa polska*, pp. 55, 56

41 Edward Dembowski, 'O postępach w filozoficznym pojmowaniu bytu,' *Rok* (1844), reprinted in *Pisma*, 4, pp. 82-7

42 Dembowski, *Pisma*, 4, p. 80. See also his 'O dążeniach dzisiejszego czasu,' *Rok* (1845), in *Pisma*, 4, pp. 385-6.

43 Dembowski, 'Tworczość w żywocie społeczności,' *Tygodnik Literacki* (1843), in *Pisma*, 3, p. 234

44 Ibid., pp. 233-7

45 Ibid., p. 239. See also his 'Kilka myśli o eklektyzmie,' *Rok* (1843), in *Pisma*, 3, pp. 357-8.

46 *Pisma*, 3, pp. 238-42

47 Dembowski, whose atheism contrasts with the religious colouring of most of the contemporary Polish Utopians, has been hailed by Polish and Russian Marxists as a precursor of 'scientific' socialism. See, for example, Przemski, *Edward Dembowski*, p. 237; Narsky, *Mirovozzrenie E. Dembovskogo,* pp. 13, 126-7.

48 Born 1808, died 1869. The most detailed account of Rzewuski's ideas is given in the unfinished history of Polish socialism in Galicia by the socialist journalist Emil Haecker's *Historja socjalizmu*, pp. 48-89. See also Bolesław Limanowski, *Historja ruchu społecznego w XIX stuleciu* (Lvov 1890), pp. 476-9; Kostołowski, *Studia*, pp. 82-4, 96, 273-7; Mogilska, *Wspólna własność ziemi* pp. 67-9; Ciołkosz, *Zarys dziejów socjalismu polskiego*, 1, pp. 347-58. Accounts by his contemporaries are to be found in the obituary by Paweł Popiel in *Czas* (Cracow), 27 Nov. 1869; Stanisław Tarnowski, 'Leon Rzewuski: Wspomnienie o pismach,' *Przegląd Polski* (Cracow), May 1870; Ludwik Dębicki, *Leon hr. Rzewuski: Wspomnienie pośmiertne* (Cracow 1870), and his *Portrety i sylwetki z dziewiętnastego stulecia*, series I (Cracow 1905), pp. 173-97. Kieniewicz, 'Do charakterystyki Leona Rzewuskiego,' prints some interesting letters from the earlier portion of Rzewuski's career. For a list (not complete)

of his published writings, see Karol Estreicher, *Bibliografia polska XIX stólecia* (Cracow), 4, (1878), pp. 159-60.

49 Kieniewicz, 'Do charakterystyki Leona Rzewuskiego,' p. 416. Cf. the comments of a later conservative colleague of Rzewuski's, Dębicki, *Portrety i sylwetki*, series I, p. 190: 'What amazement and alarm there was in the camp of the conservative gentry, and what suspicion among the radical democrats, when this descendant of Hetmans, reared in the ideas of French legitimism ... makes his début in the public arena and unfurls the standard of socialism.'

50 *Pamiętniki Pawla Popiela (1807-1892)* (Cracow 1927), p. 62; Dębicki, *Portrety i sylwetki*, I, p. 185. It is interesting to note, however, that from early manhood Rzewuski had been an admirer of Lamennais, and he continued to keep in fairly close touch with him.

51 Letter to Adam Potocki, 3 Feb. 1846, printed in Kieniewicz, 'Do charakterystyki Leona Rzewuskiego,' pp. 418, 419.

52 *Gazeta Lwowska* (Oct./Nov. 1847), no. 140, p. 928. Italics in the original.

53 See Kieniewicz, 'Sprawa włościańska w Galicji w 1848,' *Przegląd Historyczny* (Warsaw), 38 (1948), pp. 61-128, for a thorough discussion of the problems involved in emancipation and their background.

54 K. Ostaszewski-Barański, *Rok złudzeń (1848): Opowiadanie historyczne* (Złoczów n.d.), pp. 174, 175.

55 Rzewuski sct forth his views on the problem of emancipation in several leaflets published in the spring of 1848. See British Library (Reference Division), ms. 1850.c. 6 (60*); Library of the Jagiellonian University (Cracow), ms. 11959 II no. 56; Ossolineum Library (Wrocław), ms. 334.553 II. Estreicher (see n. 48) lists several items which I have been unable to trace.

56 A typical example of the hostile reaction which Rzewuski's proposals evoked among the democrats can be found in a letter from Tadeusz Wasilewski to Jan Fedorowicz, dated 3 April 1848, which is printed in a Ukrainian translation by Ivan Franko, 'Prychynky do istorii 1848 r.,' *Zapysky Naukovoho Tovarystva Imeny Shevchenka* (Lvov), 88 (1909), pt 2, p. 105. 'A coterie [of social reactionaries] is gathering here in Lvov ... Rzewuski, Potocki who is married to a Branicka.'

57 Letter dated 24 April 1848, printed in Kieniewicz, 'Do charakterstyki Leona Rzewuskiego,' pp. 422-3.

58 See Władysław Zawadzki, *Dziennikarstwo w Galicji w roku 1848* (Lvov 1878).

59 Cited below as P. The paper ran from 15 April to 29 Aug. 1848, a total of fifty-four issues appearing. It should be added that some of the articles in the Lvov organ of the Polish Democratic Society (*Dziennik Stanisławowowski*) had a distinctly socialist colouring.

60 *P.*, no. 1, p. 1. Rzewuski's articles are not usually signed in full; more often he

uses the initials: *L.R.* or *L. Rz.* Occasionally it has been possible to identify an unsigned article as his.

61 It is sometimes stated (e.g., Haecker, *Historja socjalizmu*, p. 54) that the translator was Rzewuski. This may have been so, but I have been unable to find any definite evidence of this.

62 P., no. 25, p. 95; no. 31, pp. 119-20; no. 49, pp. 198-9; no. 50, pp. 201-2.

63 See *Powody i cele Stowarzyszenia Ziemiańskiego zawiązanego dnia 3 maja 1848 przez jednego z członków.* A seven-page pamphlet by one of the leading figures in the Association, Gwalbert Pawlikowski, in the University Library in Cracow (11959 II no. 49).

64 P., no. 35, p. 137

65 P., no. 32, p. 128

66 *List do pana L. S. o socyalizmie przes L. R.* (Lvov [1848]), pp. 3, 4, 7. This short pamphlet, addressed to one of Rzewuski's opponents, Ludwik Skrzyński, was also printed as a supplement to *Gazeta Powszechna* (Lvov), 30 Sept. 1848. See also Rzewuski's letter printed in *Gazeta Lwowska*, no. 103, 1 Sept. 1848. ('The principle of socialism amounts to this, that the general good is considered as the goal and individual people as associated together for this goal. Individualism, on the other hand, regards the community as a means of securing a good living to individual people.')

67 P., no. 15, p. 206. Rzewuski's exact religious views in 1848 are not known. In his articles in *Progress* he sometimes clothed his arguments in favour of socialism in religious terms. This may have been only conventional expression, since some writers speak of his religious indifference at this period and of a spiritual awakening he underwent later, in the 1850s. There is no doubt concerning the ardent (and orthodox) Catholicism of his later years.

68 P., no. 21, pp. 79-80; *List do pana L.S.*, pp. 5-6. See also Rzewuski's letter to *Polska* (Lvov), no. 9, p. 80: 'I have not considered that [discussions] concerning property are fitting at the moment.'

69 P., no. 44, p. 178

70 P., no. 50, p. 201. Cf. Rzewuski in P., n. 54, p. 220: 'Revolution is in fact the struggle of a principle long suppressed against a social order based on an outmoded principle ... It is the violent outcome of a long-concealed intellectual development in a nation. It is the simultaneous result of the spread of faith in a new principle and of the decline of faith in the old formula of political truth.' This should be taken, however, as an objective evaluation of the facts of political life and not as qualified support on Rzewuski's part for a revolutionary solution of social problems.

71 P., no. 32, p. 123

72 P., no. 51, p. 206; no. 54, p. 220

73 P., no. 15, p. 55

74 *P.*, no. 26, p. 100; no. 49, p. 197

75 *P.*, no. 19, pp. 71-2; no. 20, p. 75; no. 32, p. 128

76 Ossolineum Library (Wrocław), ms. 334.553 II, pt II

77 See Haecker, *Historja socjalizmu*, pp. 53, 54.

78 *P.*, nos 1-3

79 *P.*, no. 11, p. 42. It should be noted that Rzewuski was far less kindly disposed to the economic demands of the big landowners of Galicia than to their political position. He was strongly opposed to any protective tariff on imported corn, considering this to be an anti-social measure. 'Cheap bread is the community's first obligation,' he wrote. 'The welfare of the consumers must not be sacrificed to the interests of the landowning class ... Let it suffice that the law guarantees them a monopoly of the land; there is no need to secure them a monopoly of production, especially where primary needs are involved. Efforts should be made so that the people may buy their bread with the smallest possible output of labour.' See *P.*, no. 14, pp. 52-3. The influence of the English liberal economists clearly influenced Rzewuski in his free trade principles – they were in direct opposition to his material interests as a big landowner. The peasants, on the other hand, though now owners of land, were still living near the subsistence level, even being threatened from time to time with famine when the harvest failed; they were therefore not yet much concerned with marketing their produce and stood on the whole to gain by free trade measures.

80 *P.*, no. 32, p. 128

81 *P.*, no. 43, p. 173

82 *P.*, no. 19, p. 72; no. 45, p. 182

83 *P.*, no. 31, p. 119; no. 52, p. 210; no. 54, p. 220

84 Dębicki, *Portrety i sylvetki*, series 1, p. 193, and his *Leon hr. Rzewuski*, p. 21

85 *P.*, no. 22, p. 86; no. 24, p. 94

86 *P.*, no. 51, p. 206. Slavdom he describes as forming 'a single race.'

87 *P.*, no. 12, pp. 43-4; no. 44, p. 80; no. 46, pp. 186-7

88 *P.*, no. 32, p. 128

89 For their situation in 1848, see Stepan Baran, *Vesna narodiv v avstro-uhors'kyi Ukraini* (Munich 1948); E.M. Kosachevskaya, *Vostochnaya Galitsiya nakanune i v period revolyutsii 1848 g.* (Lvov 1965); Maria Bohachevsky-Chomiak, *The Spring of a Nation: The Ukrainians of Eastern Galicia in 1848* (Philadelphia 1967); Mykhailo Danilak, *Halyts'ki, bukovyns'ki, zakarpats'ki ukraintsi v revoliutsii 1848-1849 rokiv* (Bratislava 1972), pp. 63-142; Jan Kozik, *Między reakcją a rewolucją: Studia z dziejów ukrainskiego ruchu narodowego w Galicji w latach 1848-1849* (Cracow 1975). See also my article 'Ivan Vahylevych (1811-1866) and the Ukrainian national identity,' *Canadian Sla-*

vonic Papers (Ottawa), 14, no. 2 (Summer 1972), pp. 153-90; reprinted in my book, *Nationalism and Populism in Partitioned Poland*, pp. 102-41.

90 A typical example of this attitude may be found in the liberal democratic National Council's appeal 'to brother Ruthenians' printed in its organ *Rada Narodowa* (Lvov), no. 16, 10 May 1848, p. 60. The Council speaks 'of our common fatherland that we call Poland.' 'The National Council,' it continued, 'does not hesitate solemnly to declare here that the rights of the Ruthenian "nationality" are equally sacred and inviolable with its own. Far from any thought of ever obstructing its free development, it considers it as just and profitable to the nation that this Ruthenian "nationality" should increase in spirit in all provinces and thus strengthen and augment the spirit of the whole nation.' With the destruction of the old unjust Poland of the gentry, the two peoples, Poles and Ruthenians, who had both suffered a like oppression under the old order, should continue as before to share a common and brighter future. 'The Ruthenian "nationality" cannot have different needs from the Polish ... Each enjoying full rights and developing in complete freedom ... will contribute the more vigorously to attaining the common welfare of the common fatherland.' Eventually all the branches of the Ruthenian people, that is to say, those across the borders under the Russians as well as in Galicia, would be joined with the Poles in a reborn Polish commonwealth based on democratic principles. 'Only the unity of all the nationalities making up Poland can usher in the triumph of the most sacred principles of mankind and constitute an impregnable base for the power and happiness of our common fatherland.'

91 *P.*, no. 18, p. 67; no. 31, p. 119; no. 38, p. 152; no. 40, p. 161; no. 41, pp. 165, 168; no. 49, p. 197

92 See *Polska* (1848), nos. 4, 6, 7, 9, 10, 11, 14, 15, 19, 21. The paper started publication in August 1848. Its reactionary views led to a strike in the Lvov printing establishments, the workmen refusing to print it. See Zawadzki, *Dziennikarstwo* (see n. 58 above), pp. 92-3.

93 A fairly restrained example is to be found in Kajetan Malecki, *Socyalizm i uwagi nad jego zasadami* (Lvov 1849), pp. 5-6. Malecki, while acknowledging that Rzewuski was quite honest and straightforward in his opinions, claims that his ideas were all 'drawn from the school of the French socialists.'

94 See *P.*, no. 53, p. 214, for some evidence that strong disagreements on policy may have arisen between Rzewuski and the editors.

95 Letter to A. Potocki, dated 11 Sept. 1848, printed in Kieniewicz, 'Do charakterystyki Leona Rzewuskiego,' p. 424.

96 Rzewuski to Amedée duc de Beauffort, letter dated 22 Dec. 1848, Polish Academy of Sciences (Cracow Branch), ms. 2408. Italics in the original.

97 Kieniewicz, 'Do charakterystyki Leona Rzewuskiego,' p. 425

98 Leaflet in British Museum, cited above in n. 55
99 In fact Rzewuski continued after 1848 to have a deep faith in the peasant commune. He still saw it as the only secure basis for democracy in a rural land, and he never ceased to proclaim his belief that a democratic state must be organized as a federation of communes. All this he felt was especially true in respect to Eastern Europe, where healthy village institutions were more essential to the well-being of society than the best conceived attempts at reshaping it from above. To some extent his alignment during the last two decades of his life with the Conservatives, who also believed *inter alia* in the virtues of communal self-government, was more a result of reframing his credo than of a fundamental change in his political and social principles. See my article 'Leon Rzewuski and the village commune.'

EPILOGUE

1 For the transitional period in the history of Polish socialism from the waning of agrarian socialism early in the 1860s to the emergence of Marxist socialism towards the end of the 1870s, see Ciolkosz, *Zarys dziejów socjalizmu polskiego*, 2. A renewed populist strand in Polish socialism of the 1870s to 1890s resulted much more from the impact of Russian *narodnichestvo* than from any lingering influence of the Polish narodniks of the pre-1863 era.
2 The writings of the Utopian socialists in the West also influenced the thinking of some of the right-wing émigrés. For instance, the former Saint-Simonian-turned-conservative Stanisław Bratkowski, who advocated collective working of the peasant's land in his book *Gmina i szkoła wiejska w Polsce* (Paris 1866, quoted in Mogilska, *Wspólna własność ziemi*, pp. 65-6), was inspired by his reading of the works of Owen and Fourier to urge the setting up of communal institutions in the villages. But at the same time of course the estates of the gentry were to remain untouched. See above, chap. 1, n. 5.
3 Władysław Kosiński, *Sprawa polska z roku 1846 przed sąd opinii publicznej wytoczona* (Poznań 1850), p. 56.

Select bibliography

Archival sources are scarce for the history of the Polish narodnik movement in the period between the November insurrection of 1830 and the January insurrection of 1863. Many documents relating to this subject were destroyed when the Rapperswil and Batignolles collections, stored in the Polish National Library, went up in flames during the German bombardment of Warsaw in September 1939. The archival materials still extant, whether in Poland or abroad, tend to throw light on personalities and organization rather than on ideology, which is the main subject of this book. However, for the 'prehistory' of the first Polish revolutionary populist society, the Polish People, there are important manuscripts in the Bibliothèque Polonaise in Paris. I have printed selections from these in my book of source materials, *Geneza Ludu Polskiego w Anglii* (and further references to unpublished documents are made in the notes). In a contribution to the Warsaw historical journal, *Przegląd Historyczny* (1961) I also printed a long document which throws an interesting light on the Polish People's later ideology. In addition, some rare items relating to the London Commune of the second half of the 1850s have been published in *Przegląd Historyczny*, by I.S. Miller (1959) and F. Romaniukowa (1960). Recently V.A. D'iakov, like Miller a scholar from the Soviet Union, discovered in the Central State Military-Historical Archives in Moscow a large collection of documents which deal with the activities and ideas of Father Ściegienny. A selection from them has been appended to the Polish translation of his book (1972).

The list printed below gives the more important items published during this century on Polish agrarian socialism of the 1830s to 1850s.

BACZKO, BRONISŁAW, ed. *Towarzystwo Demokratyczne Polskie: Dokumenty i pisma.* Warsaw 1954

BALICKA, ZOFJA. 'Legenda o ks. Piotrze Ściegiennym.' *Insurrekcje* (Warsaw), no. 3 (1930)

BARTEL, WOJCIECH M. 'Rewolucja krakowska 1846 roku na tle niektórych polskich koncepcji społeczno-politycznych lat 1831-1846.' *Czasopismo Prawno-Historyczne* (Warsaw), 9 (1957), no. 1

BARTKOWSKI, JAN. *Wspomnienia z powstania 1831 roku i pierwszych lat emigracji,* ed. Eugeniusz Sawrymowicz. Cracow 1966

BENDER, RYSZARD. *Chrześcijanie w polskich ruchach demokratycznych XIX stulecia.* Warsaw 1975

BOREJSZA, JERZY W. 'Le socialisme polonais en 1831-1871'. In *Le centenaire de la Commune de Paris: Le socialisme français de l'Europe Centrale (Les Cahiers de Varsovie).* Warsaw 1972

BROCK, PETER. 'The birth of Polish socialism.' *Journal of Central European Affairs* (Boulder, Colorado), 13 (1953), no. 3

- *Geneza Ludu Polskiego w Anglii: Materiały żródłowe.* London 1962[GLP]

- 'Leon Rzewuski and the village commune.' *Slavic Review* (Seattle), 22 (1963), no. 4

- 'Na marginesie historii Gromady Grudziąż.' *Przegląd Historyczny* (Warsaw), 52 (1961), nos 1 and 2

- *Nationalism and Populism in Partitioned Poland: Selected Essays.* London 1973

- 'The Polish revolutionary commune in London,' *Slavonic and East European Review* (London), 35 (1956), no. 84

- 'Polish socialists in early Victorian England: three documents.' *Polish Review* (New York), 6 (1961), no. 1/2

- *Z dziejów Wielkiej Emigracji w Anglii.* Warsaw 1958

- 'Zeno Świętosławski, a Polish forerunner of the *narodniki.*' *American Slavic and East European Review* (New York), 13 (1954), no. 4

CIOŁKOSZ, LIDIA and ADAM. *Zarys dziejów socjalizmu polskiego* (London). 1 (1966), 2 (1972)

CYGLER, BOGUSŁAW. *Działalnosc polityczno-społeczna Joachima Lelewela na emigracji w latach 1831-1861.* Gdańsk 1969

- *Zjednoczenie Emigracji Polskiej 1837-1846.* Gdańsk 1963

DEMBOWSKI, EDWARD. *Pisma,* ed. Anna Śladkowska and Maria Żmigrodzka. 5 vols. Warsaw 1955

D'IAKOV, V.A. *Piotr Ściegienny i jego spuścizna,* tr. by Jerzy Skowronek. Warsaw 1972

- et al., eds. *Russko-pol'skie revoliutsionnye sviazi 60-kh godov i vossta-nie 1863 goda.* Moscow 1962

DROBNER, BOLESŁAW. *Mickiewicz jako socjalista.* Warsaw 1947.

DUKER, ABRAHAM G. 'Polish *Emigré* Christian Socialists on the Jewish problem.' *Jewish Social Studies* (New York), 14 (1952), no. 4

GĄSIOROWSKA, NATALIA, ed. *W stulecie Wiosny Ludów, 1848-1948.* Warsaw, 3 (1951), 4 (1951), 5 (1953)

GRONIOWSKI, KRZYSZTOF. *Problem rewolucji agrarnej w ideologii obozów politycznych w latach 1846-1870.* Warsaw 1957

HAECKER, EMIL. *Historja socjalizmu w Galicji i na Śląsku cieszyńskim* (Cracow). 1 (1933)

KALEMBKA, SŁAWOMIR. *Wielka emigracja: Polskie wychodźstwo poli-tyczne w latach 1831-1862.* Warsaw 1971

KAMIEŃSKI, HENRYK. *Wybór pism,* ed. I. Bibrowska. Warsaw 1953

KIENIEWICZ, STEFAN. 'Do charakterystyki Leona Rzewuskiego (1841-1848).' *Roczniki Historyczne* (Poznań), 17 (1948), no. 2

- *The Emancipation of the Polish Peasantry.* Chicago and London 1969
- *Legion Mickiewicza, 1848-1849.* Warsaw 1955

KNAPOWSKA, WISŁAWA. 'Lud Polski – Gromada Rewolucyjna Londyn.' *Kwartalnik Historyczny* (Warsaw), 62 (1955), no. 2

KOBERDOWA, IRENA. *Wyodrębnianie się nurtu socjalistycznego w środow-isku polskiej emigracji w latach 1848-1863.* Warsaw 1964

KOSTOŁOWSKI, ERAZM. *Studia nad kwestią włościańską w latach 1846-1864 ze szczególnym uwzględnieniem literatury politycznej.* Lvov 1938

KRÓLIKOWSKI, LUDWIK. *Wybór pism,* ed. Adam Sikora and Hanna Tem-kinowa. Warsaw 1972

KRYSANKA, HALINA. 'Z dziejów Gromady Grudziąż Ludu Polskiego.' *Studia z Dziejów Myśli Społecznej i Kwestii Robotniczej w XIX Wieku* (Warsaw), no. 1 (1964)

ŁADYKA, JERZY. *Dembowski.* Warsaw 1968

LIMANOWSKI, BOLESŁAW. *Stanisław Worcell,* 2d ed. Cracow 1948

ŁUKASZEWICZ, WITOLD. *Tadeusz Krępowiecki: żolnierz-rewolucjonista.* Warsaw 1954

- 'Trybuna Ludów.' *Prace Polonistyczne* (Wrocław), 11 (1953)

MŁYNARSKI, ZYGMUNT. *W kręgu sprawy ks. Piotra Ściegiennego.* Warsaw 1961

MOGILSKA, HANNA. *Wspólna własność ziemi w polskiej publicystyce lat 1835-1860.* Warsaw 1949

MIKOS, STANISŁAW. *Gromady Ludu Polskiego w Anglii 1835-1846.* Gdańsk 1962

- 'W sprawie składu społecznego i genezy ideologii Gromad Ludu Polskiego w Anglii 1835-1846.' *Przegląd Historyczny* (Warsaw), 51 (1960), no. 4
MILLER, I.S. 'Dokoła genezy Gromady Rewolucyjnej Londyn.' *Przegląd Historyczny* (Warsaw), 50 (1959), no. 4
NARSKY, I.S. *Mirovozzrenie E. Dembovskogo: Iz istorii pol'skoy filozofii XIX v.* Moscow 1954
PRZEMSKI, LEON. *Edward Dembowski.* Warsaw 1953
PODOLECKI, JAN KANTY. *Wybór pism z lat 1846-1856,* ed. Andrzej Grodek. Warsaw 1955
PONIATOWSKI, ZYGMUNT. *O poglądach społeczno-filozoficznych Henryka Kamieńskiego.* Warsaw 1955
ROMANIUKOWA, FELICJA. 'Dalsze dokumenty do historii Gromady Rewolucyjnej Londyn.' *Przegląd Historyczny* (Warsaw), 51 (1960), no. 3
RZADKOWSKA, HELENA. *Działalność Centralizacji londynskiej Towarzystwa Demokratycznego Polskiego 1850-1862.* Wrocław 1972
SIKORA, ADAM. ed. *Gromady Ludu Polskiego.* Warsaw 1974
ŚLADKOWSKA, ANNA. *Poglądy społeczno-polityczne i filozoficzne Edwarda Dembowskiego.* Warsaw 1955
STECKA, M. *Edward Dembowski.* Lvov 1911
SZPOTAŃSKI, STANISŁAW. 'Emigracja polska w Anglii (1831-1848).' *Biblioteka Warszawska* (Warsaw), 204, pt 2 (1909)
- *Lud Polski (Z dziejów polskiej myśli socjalistycznej).* Lvov 1907
TEMKINOWA, HANNA. *Gromady Ludu Polskiego (Zarys ideologii).* Warsaw 1962
- ed. *Lud Polski: Wybór dokumentów.* Warsaw 1957
La Tribune des peuples, ed. Władysław Mickiewicz. Paris 1907; phototype edition, Wrocław 1963
TUROWSKI, JAN. *Utopia społeczna Ludwika Królikowskiego 1799-1878.* Warsaw 1958
TYROWICZ, MARIAN. *Prawda i mit w biografii Juliana Macieja Goslara 1820-1852.* Warsaw 1973
- *Sprawa ks. Piotra Ściegiennego.* Warsaw 1949
- *Z dziejów polskich ruchów społecznych w XIX wieku.* London 1965
VALENTA, JAROSLAV. 'Petr Ściegienny a radikalní rolnické hnutí v Polsku koncem první poloviny 19 století.' *Slovanské Historické Studie* (Prague), 8 (1971)
WYCECH, CZESŁAW. *Ks. Piotr Ściegienny: Zarys programu społecznego i wybór pism.* Warsaw 1953
- *Z przeszłości ruchów chłopskich (1768-1861).* Warsaw 1952

WAJSBLUM, MAREK. 'Od Belwederu do Leominster.' *Wiadomości* (London), 13 Jan. 1952 (no. 302)

WEINTRAUB, WIKTOR. 'Adam Mickiewicz, the mystic politician.' *Harvard Slavic Studies* (Cambridge Mass.), 1 (1953)

ZAKRZEWSKI, BOHDAN. *Tygodnik Literacki 1838-1845*. Warsaw 1964

– 'Z dziejów walki o ideologię demokratyczną w Poznaniu w latach 1830-1850.' *Przegląd Zachodni* (Poznań), 1953, no. 6/8

ŻYCHOWSKI, MARIAN. *Polska myśl socjalistyczna XIX i XX wieku (do 1918 r.)*. Warsaw 1976 (This volume reached me too late for consideration above.)

Index

CENTRE FOR RUSSIAN AND EAST EUROPEAN STUDIES
University of Toronto

Feeding the Russian Fur Trade by James R. Gibson. (University of Wisconsin Press, Madison, Wisconsin, 1969)

The Czech Renascence of the Nineteenth Century edited by Peter Brock and H. Gordon Skilling. (University of Toronto Press, Toronto, 1970)

The Soviet Wood-Processing Industry: a linear programming analysis of the role of transportation costs in location and flow patterns by Brenton M. Barr. (University of Toronto Press, Toronto, 1970)

Interest Groups in Soviet Politics edited by H. Gordon Skilling and Franklyn Griffiths. (Princeton University Press, Princeton, New Jersey, 1971)

Between Gogol' and Ševčenko by George S. N. Luckyj. (Harvard Series in Ukrainian Studies. Wilhelm Fink Verlag, Munich, Germany, 1971)

The Collective Farm in Soviet Agriculture by Robert C. Stuart. (D. C. Heath and Company, Lexington, Mass., 1972)

Narrative Modes in Czech Literature by Lubomir Dolezel. (University of Toronto Press, Toronto, 1973)

Leon Trotsky and the Politics of Economic Isolation by Richard B. Day. (Cambridge University Press, Cambridge, England, 1973)

Literature and Ideology in Soviet Education by Norman Shneidman. (D. C. Heath and Company, Lexington, Mass., 1973)

Guide to the Decisions of the Communist Party of the Soviet Union, 1917-1967 by Robert H. McNeal. (University of Toronto Press, Toronto, 1974)

Resolutions and Decisions of the Communist Party of the Soviet Union 1898-1964 General Editor, Robert H. McNeal. Four Volumes. (University of Toronto Press, Toronto, 1974)

The Slovak National Awakening: an essay in the intellectual history of east central Europe by Peter Brock. (University of Toronto Press, Toronto, 1976)

Czechoslovakia's Interrupted Revolution by H. Gordon Skilling. (Princeton University Press, Princeton, New Jersey, 1976)

The Russian Revolution: a study in mass mobilization by John L. H. Keep. (Weidenfield and Nicolson, London, 1976; W. W. Norton and Co., New York, 1977)